CONTENTS

ISBN 1-898837-60-0

Economics & Business Studies Update is compiled by Gary Cook
and produced by Elizabeth Cook.

Printed by Wyke Printers Ltd, Kingston-upon-Hull.

**Published by Hidcote Press,
60 Mill Rise, Swanland, East Yorkshire HU14 3PW.**

Further copies of ***Economics & Business Studies Update 2002*** may be purchased from this address. Further details are given on page 64.

e-mail enquiries to: hidcotepress@tinyonline.co.uk

HOW TO USE THIS UPDATE

Economics & Business Studies Update is designed to fill the gaps in students' knowledge between textbooks (which are often dated) and the latest events and policies.

By reading and rereading ***Economics & Business Studies Update*** students will benefit in several ways:

EXAM PREPARATION: Grades can be improved by introducing up-to-date knowledge into examination answers. Familiarity with the data used, the graphical presentations and the informative commentary will assist effective examination preparation.

COURSEWORK: ***Economics & Business Studies Update*** is an affordable resource which can be purchased by every student and used regularly to inform class discussion and improve performance in essays and assignments.

INTERVIEWS: Candidates will be able to impress interviewers with their knowledge of "real world" issues obtained from ***Economics & Business Studies Update*** - the most up-to-date and affordable students' guide to business and the economy.

ABOUT THE AUTHOR

Gary Cook has taught both Economics and Business Studies for many years and has published student ***"Updates"*** since the 1980s. He is currently the Director of Commercial Partnerships at the University of Lincoln.

THE EURO

On 1st January 2002 the new euro notes and coins entered into circulation amongst the twelve participating member states. After a short dual-currency period of two months national currencies such as the French franc and the German mark will be phased out, and all but three of the EU member states (Denmark, Sweden and the UK) will have their long awaited ***single currency.***

The change over to euro notes and coins is the latest stage in a complex process which began over forty years ago:

1957: France, West Germany, Italy, Belgium, the Netherlands and Luxembourg sign the Treaty of Rome establishing the European Economic Community (EEC).

1973: UK, Ireland and Denmark join.

1980s: Greece, Spain and Portugal join. EEC becomes the European Community (EC).

1987: The Single European Act is passed, paving the way for the development of a free trade zone (The Single European Market) with a progressive phasing out of frontier controls.

1991: Maastricht Treaty negotiated which sets out a timetable for the introduction of a single European currency. The UK and Denmark "opt out" of the final stages of this process, giving themselves the right to decide later. The European Community to be retitled European Union (EU).

1993: The Single European Market comes into official existence.

1995: Austria, Finland and Sweden join the EU, increasing the membership to its current level of fifteen countries.

1999: The Eurozone is formed. Eleven countries lock together their exchange rates irrevocably and the euro is formed as a "virtual" currency. Businesses begin to adopt dual pricing in local currency and euros. People hold euro bank accounts but continue to use the old national notes and coins.

2000: The Danish population vote ***no*** to the euro in a referendum and choose to keep their national currency, the krone.

2002: Euro notes and coins are issued in the Eurozone twelve, and national currencies cease to circulate.

A much fuller account of this process is given in ***The Single European Currency - 2000 Edition - a students' guide*** by Gary Cook. Details of how to order this publication are given on page 63.

IMPLICATIONS OF THE EURO FOR BRITAIN

Britain is not in the Eurozone, but it is part of the Single European Market. This created a zone of 365 million people in which there is free trade in goods and services and free movement of capital and labour. The idea was to break down the barriers to trade and economic integration so that market forces could operate more effectively.

British exporters benefit from the Single European Market. They can sell to customers in any EU country on the basis of quality and price competitiveness without any restrictions. Even the cost of transport has been reduced, with improved road and rail infrastructure and minimal or non-existent delays at border crossing points.

The introduction of the euro does, however, undermine the ***level playing field*** of the Single Market for those countries which have decided to stay out. A business in Belgium, for example, can now buy its components and supplies from any one of the twelve Eurozone countries in its own currency - the euro. To buy the same products from Britain, Denmark or Sweden involves: calculating the cost in euros; bearing foreign exchange costs to exchange euros for sterling, the krone or krona; and a risk that exchange rates might change during the period between the placing of an order and the final delivery of the contract.

British exporters are increasingly likely to have to bear these costs. If they expect their Eurozone customers to do so, they may well lose business and market share. The implications for the serious exporter to the Eurozone are:

- They will need to produce catalogues and price lists marked up in euros.
- They will need to open euro bank accounts and accept payment in euros as well as their own local currency.
- They will bear the foreign exchange risk. For example, an order for £1000 worth of goods might be accepted by a British firm from a Eurozone customer at a time when £1 = 1.60 euros. The price quoted is 1000 x 1.60 = 1,600 euros. Before payment falls due the euro weakens to £1 = 1.70 euros. The British supplier receives the agreed 1600 euros, but this is now worth 1600 ÷ 1.70 = £941.
- Companies in the UK can insure or "hedge" against currency fluctuations, but this also involves costs for the services of financial institutions.

TOURISM: Surveys of British hoteliers show that they are keen for Britain to join the euro. They know that visitors from the Eurozone will expect to see prices quoted in euros, and will be disappointed if their new currency is not accepted here. Some tourist attractions have said they will accept payment in euros. Historic Royal Palaces, for example, which runs Hampton Court, Kensington Palace and the Tower of London, will accept euros from spring 2002. British holidaymakers going abroad will quickly encounter the euro, and will see real benefits if they tour from one Eurozone country to another. Once they have changed their money into euros they will be able to spend it in any one of the twelve member countries. Some analysts believe this will make more British people want to see the euro introduced here. Major UK retailers such as Boots, Marks & Spencer, Virgin, W H Smith, John Lewis and Safeway, are preparing to accept euros, initially at stores in popular tourist areas. Some people have dubbed this ***euro creep*** - a process by which the euro gradually becomes used as a parallel currency to the pound, and becomes more acceptable to the public as a result.

INVESTMENT: Britain has, for several years, been the most popular country in the EU for foreign direct investment in factories and other business operations. There is little sign yet, but some economists believe that the longer we stay outside of the Eurozone the more likely new investors will be to locate their investments in other countries using the euro.

POLITICS: Britain was slow to join the EEC and missed out on the benefits enjoyed by the founding members, which prospered greatly during the early years after it was formed. When we did join, we were obliged to accept the institutional arrangements for running the EEC, over which we had little influence. Some politicians fear we are repeating the same mistake with the euro. By staying out, we look as if we are in the 'slow lane' of European integration and our influence over EU policy might eventually suffer.

BENEFITS OF STAYING OUT

The question over whether Britain should join the Eurozone is, of course, very controversial. By staying out we benefit in a number of ways :

SOVEREIGNTY: Adoption of a single currency would mean that power to conduct an independent monetary policy, to control interest rates and to devalue would shift from the British parliament and the Bank of England to European institutions over which we have little control. Euro-sceptic Conservative MPs such as John Redwood have been the most outspoken critics of this potential loss of sovereignty, but their views on this issue are thought to be shared by some Labour MPs. Once we have adopted a European rather than British currency and monetary policy, sceptics argue, pressure will mount for further integration of our individual economies through common fiscal policies and social legislation. A bigger role for the European parliament and institutions means, in their eyes, an unacceptable loss of British influence and independence.

INTEREST RATES: The Bank of England was given operational independence from the government in 1997, and so far this has proved to be a good decision. The Bank has been able to adjust interest rates to suit economic conditions in the UK and has managed to stabilise the economy, maintain respectable rates of economic growth, and keep inflation under control. In fact, the Bank of England has been far more successful in doing this than governments were in the past when they controlled interest rates. Many people think that it would be a pity to take this power away again and put control of interest rates into the hands of the European Central Bank (ECB) - especially as this new institution has frequently been criticised for inept management of European interest rates.

THE WEAK EURO: Members of the Eurozone benefit from internal monetary stability. Since 1999 their exchange rates have been fixed, and from 2002 they each use exactly the same currency. The same advantages of stability have ***not*** applied to euro exchange rates with other parts of the world.

The euro has lost nearly 30% of its value against the US dollar, largely because of the relative underperformance of Eurozone economies and the lack of confidence in ECB policies. If Britain had joined the euro at the outset in 1999, it would have seen more exchange rate stability against European currencies, but ***less*** stability against the dollar.

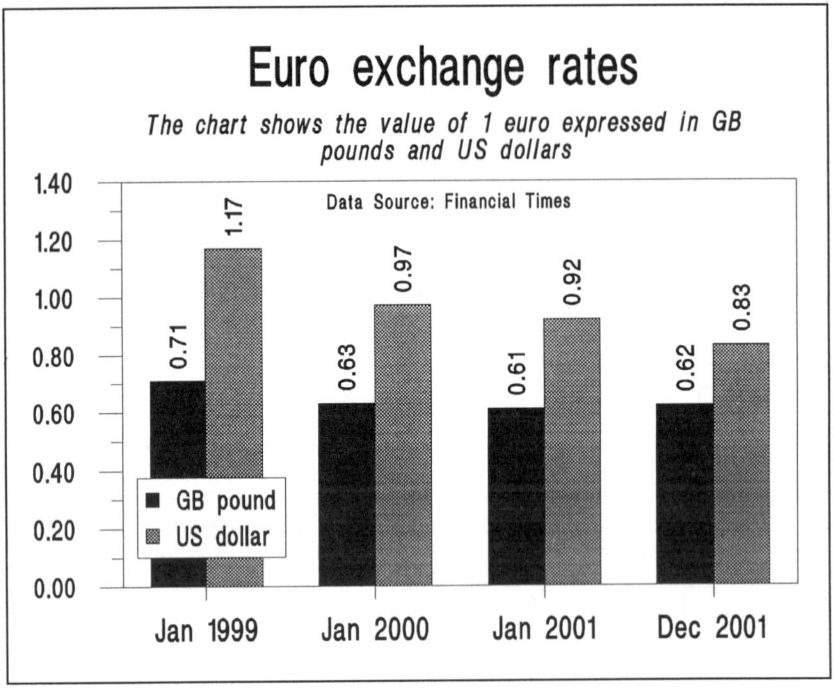

WEATHERING RECESSION: During recent years the British Chancellor of the Exchequer, Gordon Brown, has made macroeconomic stability one of his primary objectives. He has so far avoided the ***boom and bust*** failures of his predecessors, and there is a good deal of optimism that Britain (free to pursue its own economic policies) is poised to weather the world recession rather better than the USA and the Eurozone economies.

BRITAIN'S POSITION ON THE EURO

The official stance of Britain's Labour government is to back British membership of the euro in principle. It has adopted a 'prepare and decide' strategy. A decision will be taken during the next few years whether or not to

recommend Euro entry to the British people. The government says it will base its recommendation on five economic tests.

THE FIVE ECONOMIC TESTS FOR UK MEMBERSHIP OF THE EURO

1. Convergence between Britain and the economies of the single currency must be sustainable.
2. Sufficient flexibility should exist in the new currency system to cope with economic change.
3. The effect on investment must be favourable.
4. Britain's financial services industry (particularly the City of London) must benefit.
5. The single currency must be good for UK employment.

If all five tests are passed, the government says that it would hold a referendum asking the electorate to vote on this single issue - whether Britain should scrap the pound and join the Eurozone.

The timing of such a referendum is by no means clear cut. Some people thought that the Labour landslide victory in the 2001 general election would bring a quick vote on the euro, but this is clearly not to be. This remains one of the most uncertain areas of UK economic policy as the following headlines reveal:

* ***British backing for EU at lowest for twenty years*** (Guardian, 25 July 2000) - Opinion polls revealed that only 26% of Britons thought that the EU is 'a good thing', and only 22% support the euro.
* ***Blair delivers most cautious verdict yet on euro membership*** (Financial Times, 20 October 2000) - Speaking in the year before the general election, the Prime Minister said that if an opinion poll asked him whether he wanted to join the euro today, he would say 'no', but favoured membership in principle once the five economic tests were met.
* ***Blair agrees timing for euro vote*** (Guardian, 27 July 2001) - With the election safely behind them, Tony Blair and Gordon Brown, his Chancellor, were said to be planning a referendum in 2002 or 2003.
* ***Euro: the pieces come together*** (Sunday Times, 7 October 2001) - Following the September 11 terrorist attacks on America, Tony Blair had said 'round the world nations are instinctively drawing together'. He appeared to link this search for solidarity and security with renewed interest in joining the euro. In a technical feature, the Sunday Times Economics Editor, David Smith, pointed to statistics which appeared to show UK convergence with the Eurozone on economic growth and interest rates. This would allow UK entry to go ahead if there was the political will to do so.
* ***UK not ready for euro, say ex-Treasury chiefs*** (Sunday Times, 4 November 2001) - The Chancellor's current advisers had confirmed that a thorough assessment of the UK's readiness to join the euro would be complete by June 2003 at the latest. A report commissioned by New Europe and Business for Sterling (groups which oppose the

euro) said that the five tests could not be met within the next two years. A queue of former Treasury 'mandarins', led by Sir Alan Budd (government chief economist 1991-1997), formed to endorse the report and argue against entry during the present parliament.

* ***PM blows hot on euro vote but declines to set date*** (Guardian 24 November 2001) - In his most pro-euro speech ever, Tony Blair argued the case for drawing closer to Europe. He referred to the history of 'missed opportunities' in Britain's dealings with Europe, but refused to give the slightest hint over the prospective timing of a referendum.

Whilst this uncertainty persists, readers would be well advised to look out for further news coverage which may point towards a possible decision date. Also, though there is no easy answer to the question ***should the UK join?***, students should review all of the arguments for and against and form their own opinion on this important issue.

THE WORLD ECONOMY

For students of Economics and Business Studies, following trends in the world economy has never been more important. Economists have used this term over many years, but it is only in recent decades that the barriers to trade have fallen sufficiently to give this term real meaning. As trade has expanded and ***globalisation*** has taken place, individual economies have become more and more interconnected. Consequently, events in one part of the world are more likely to affect us all. It is not sufficient to study national economic conditions - we really do need to take a world view.

INTERNATIONAL MONETARY FUND (IMF)

The International Monetary Fund (www.imf.org) monitors and assesses developments in the global economy. Over recent months the IMF has downgraded its estimates for world economic growth to 2.4% in 2001, compared with 4.7% in 2000. This assessment was made after the September 11 attacks on New York and Washington, and points to a world economy on the brink of recession.

The slowdown in economic growth in 2001 (forecast to continue in 2002) has been widespread, affecting all geographical areas. Developing Countries and Countries in Transition appear, on the surface, to be less affected, but they are so far behind in terms of wealth and prosperity that a rapid growth rate is needed if they are ever to show any signs of catching up.

The downturn in the major advanced industrial economies is particularly worrying. These represent a large part of world Gross Domestic Product (GDP) and are also the biggest markets for products made elsewhere. Also, the downturn facing these economies is synchronised for the first time since the 1970s. During the intervening period, weakness in some economies has tended to be offset by strength elsewhere. A good example was the Asian crisis in 1998 when Japan and the "tiger" economies, such as South Korea

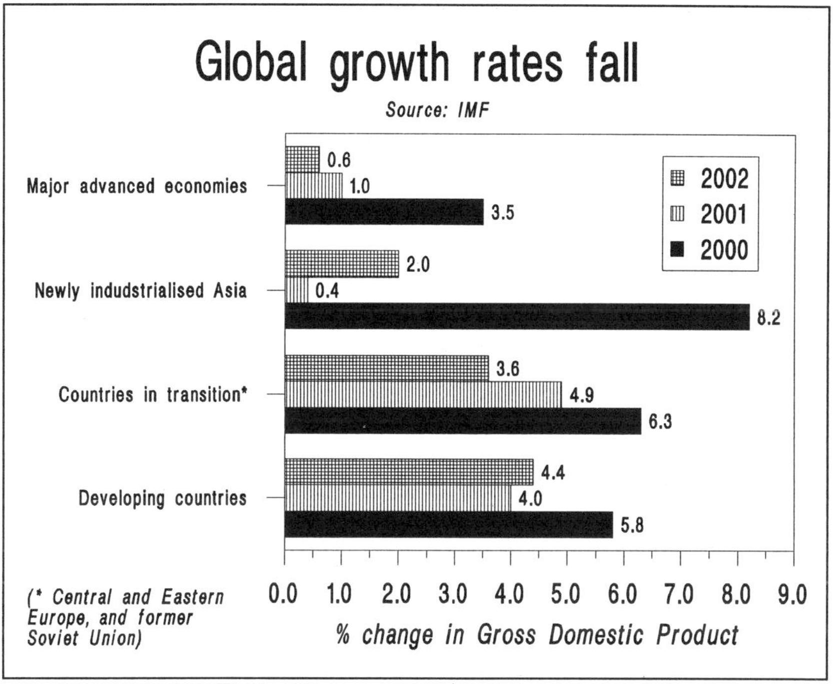
Global growth rates fall
Source: IMF
Major advanced economies
Newly indudstrialised Asia
Countries in transition*
Developing countries
0.6
1.0
3.5
2.0
0.4
8.2
3.6
4.9
6.3
4.4
4.0
5.8
2002
2001
2000
0.0 1.0 2.0 3.0 4.0 5.0 6.0 7.0 8.0 9.0
% change in Gross Domestic Product
(* Central and Eastern Europe, and former Soviet Union)

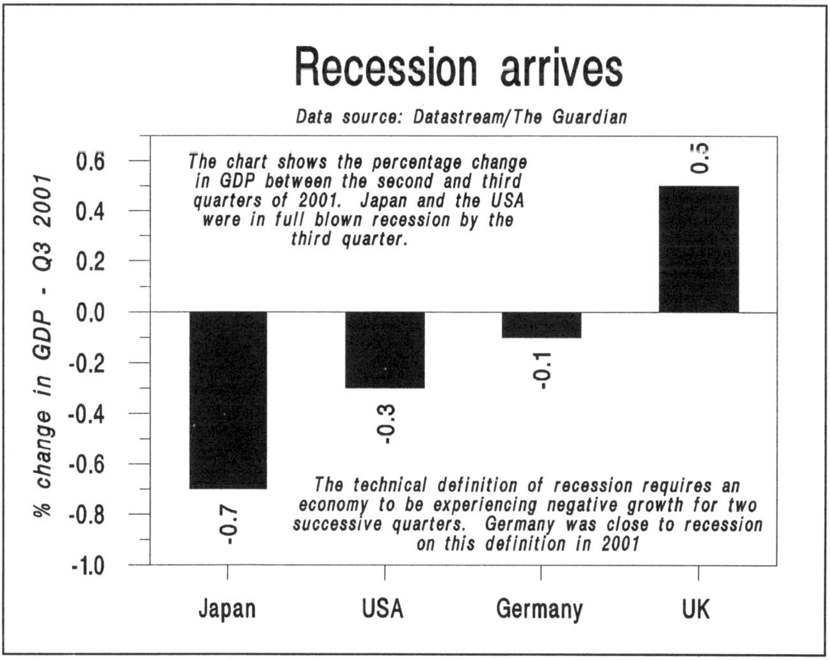
Recession arrives
Data source: Datastream/The Guardian
% change in GDP - Q3 2001
0.6
0.4
0.2
0.0
-0.2
-0.4
-0.6
-0.8
-1.0
The chart shows the percentage change in GDP between the second and third quarters of 2001. Japan and the USA were in full blown recession by the third quarter.
-0.7
-0.3
-0.1
0.5
The technical definition of recession requires an economy to be experiencing negative growth for two successive quarters. Germany was close to recession on this definition in 2001
Japan
USA
Germany
UK

and Taiwan, slumped. Growth proved so powerful and resilient in the USA (and to a lesser extent the other mature industrial economies) that a global recession was avoided. The Asian economies recovered more quickly than most economists had dared to hope, and the ease with which they could export to booming North America generated renewed growth. Synchronised recessions work differently, with weakness in a group of large and powerful economies dragging each other downward. Economic weakness on this scale can be "contagious". Growth in economies which previously looked healthy turns downward - usually because of a slump in export markets.

Within the major advanced economies, the USA, Japan and Germany have shown the greatest weakness in 2001. These are the three largest economies in the world and they are all in or close to recession.

UNITED STATES OF AMERICA

The USA has often been referred to as the ***locomotive of world growth.*** This description was particularly appropriate during the 1990s, when a powerful US boom occurred which was fuelled by stock market gains, low import prices and heavy investment in new technology. In the second half of the decade annual GDP growth averaged between 4% and 5% - a blistering rate of expansion for a mature industrial economy such as the USA.

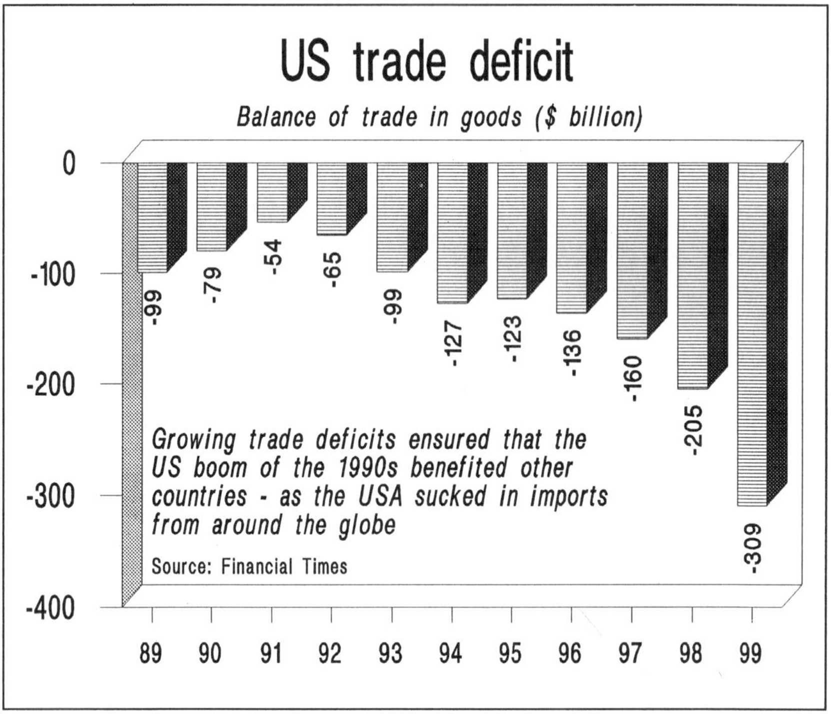

A balanced pattern of growth would have seen a rapid expansion of imports matched by buoyant exports during this growth phase. This was not the case. A huge trade ***imbalance*** set in, which can be illustrated by the chart. The US trade deficit ballooned upwards as imports were sucked in to meet the ever-increasing needs of the booming economy.

As 2001 dawned it was becoming increasingly evident that the boom was over. During the previous year the NASDAQ index of technology stocks had crashed as dot.coms and other hi-tech companies failed. Unemployment began to build up and confidence in the US economy wavered. It was clear long before September 11 that growth was decelerating, and the only question being asked was whether a full blown recession was on the way. Speaking a fortnight after the terrorist attack, the IMF's chief economist said that recession in America was now a ***done deal,*** though he later tried to retract this remark because of potential further damage to consumer and investor confidence. US economists, with the benefit of hindsight, now think that recession did actually start in the second quarter of 2001.

Opinions differ about the likely duration of a US recession. Optimists, such as Treasury Secretary Paul O'Neill, have stressed the underlying strength of the US economy and predict a "V" shaped growth path, with rapid recovery in prospect. Pessimists fear that the imbalances will need longer to unwind. Many US businesses have over-invested in plant and equipment. Consumers have become progressively more and more indebted as they binged on credit and ran down their savings. A more frugal period in which savings are restored and investment is reduced might be needed before rapid growth can resume.

GERMANY

Germany has often been referred to as ***Europe's powerhouse.*** It is an economic giant which accounts for one third of the total output of the twelve Eurozone economies. Germany, with 80 million inhabitants, is one of the most populous European countries, and it achieved its economic muscle through a post-war ***economic miracle*** in which it reconstructed itself as a vibrant manufacturing success. More recently, however, the giant has stumbled, and German growth has been slower than that of its European neighbours for the following reasons:

- Re-unification of East and West Germany in the late 1980s led to an initial boom, but then stagnation as the prosperous West groaned under the higher taxes and debt required to finance the modernisation and subsidised living standards of the East.
- Previously successful export industries, such as capital equipment, have suffered recently because of worldwide over-capacity and falling demand.
- Germany has a larger manufacturing sector overall than most other advanced economies, leaving it very exposed to falling exports in times of world recession.

- Consumer confidence has been so weak that retail sales have suffered. Experts blame worries over the state of German industry and mistrust of the euro, which is seen by many Germans as a poor substitute for the deutschemark.
- German employers are hampered by very high labour costs and restrictive employment laws which make it very difficult to sack workers if business conditions deteriorate. Many manufacturers, such as Grundig, famous for its TV sets and other electrical goods, are switching production to Austria which is seen as a lower cost location.

Germany grew slowly in the 1990s, and if it under-performs in the current decade, the world's third largest economy could be overtaken by France and the UK.

JAPAN

Japan, once the model of industrial efficiency, has suffered a decade of stagnation and four periods of technical recession, with falling GDP. As well as falling output, land prices have fallen for nine years in a row, and the Nikkei index of leading shares barely stands above a quarter of its value during the boom years of the late 1980s. Even retail prices are falling - a condition referred to as ***deflation.*** Consumers have effectively gone on strike, refusing to buy products which will almost certainly cost less in a few months' time.

During Japan's recession unemployment has risen steadily to around 5% of the workforce, and consumer confidence has been shredded as company after company has had to abandon their policy of guaranteed jobs for life.

Japanese banks are particularly shaky. They have huge amounts of bad debt from loans to companies which will never be able to repay them. Nobody is certain how deep this problem goes. The Japanese government says that the banks need to write off 18 trillion yen ($144 billion) but Nomura, a Japanese bank, says that the true figure is 200 trillion yen ($1.6 trillion).

The public finances of Japan are no better. Since 1992 there have been no less than ten major ***stimulus packages*** - huge increases in public spending to try to kick start economic growth. Each one failed, and now the Japanese government has the world's largest public debt, equivalent to 130% of annual GDP.

The failure of the Japanese economy to respond to economic policy is truly alarming. As well as the fiscal stimuli mentioned above, official interest rates have been set at, or close to, zero for several years - with no discernible effect on consumption or growth.

With Japan's domestic economy totally stagnant, the potential damage it could suffer from a serious world recession is immense. Buoyant export demand, particularly to the USA, has prevented even more serious economic problems in the past, but the slowdown in world growth increases Japan's difficulties.

THE TERRORIST ATTACK ON AMERICA

The attacks by terrorists on New York and Washington and the subsequent military action against Afghanistan by the USA and Britain adds a further dimension of uncertainty which has accentuated the slide into a world recession. The ***full*** effects of these terrible events on the world economy will not be known for some time to come, but history does give some clues.

During the late twentieth century, wars had major effects on the world economy.

YOM KIPPUR WAR 1973: Israel and its Arab neighbours went to war at a time when the global economy was slowing and the US economy was already contracting. The war caused massive disruption to oil supplies and a quadrupling of crude oil prices. The huge increase in costs and more general inflationary effects worsened the world recession and prolonged it well into 1974.

GULF WAR 1990: When Iraqi tanks rolled into Kuwait, and war with the USA and its allies appeared inevitable, the world price of oil soared from nearly $15 to $40 a barrel. This war also started as recession was looming, and such a violent hike in oil prices was a serious blow. However, it was very short-lived. Most of the members of the Organisation of Petroleum Exporting Countries (OPEC) allied with the USA on this occasion, and as the oil taps of Kuwait and Iraq were turned off by military blockades the other oil exporters increased their supplies. Oil prices quickly sank back to pre-invasion levels. The main economic effect of the Gulf War was a fall in business and consumer confidence in the leading economies, which contributed towards recession.

WAR AGAINST TERRORISM

The recent crisis is different in many ways from earlier conflicts. It started without warning on September 11. It had a military dimension - starting with the bombing and ground troop operations in Afghanistan. Crucially, it involved serious casualties and damage in the USA - the world's largest economy. Western leaders have warned that the ***war against terrorism*** will be long, possibly lasting for years, and will be fought on many fronts. As if to re-emphasise America's vulnerability to terrorism, Washington, New Jersey and Miami were quickly affected by lethal anthrax attacks - the first successful acts of bio-terrorism to affect the Western world.

Whilst the aggregate effects of these shocks might be difficult to predict, it is possible to identify some important immediate consequences of this crisis.

AIRLINES: The sight on television screens of hijacked passenger jets crashing into the twin towers of the World Trade Centre, New York, caused a dramatic collapse in confidence in the safety of air travel. Furthermore, in times of international trouble, travellers feel vulnerable in many parts of the world and stay at home instead. The consequences for the airline industry have been severe, with transatlantic traffic initially cut by over 30%. British Airways promptly cut 7,000 jobs from its workforce, and in the USA 100,000 airline workers were laid off.

INSURANCE: The damage caused by the terrorist attacks on the World Trade Centre destroyed much of the heart of New York's financial district - one of the most valuable office developments in the world. Around 3,000 people were killed. Insurance claims are expected to reach $100 billion, the largest in history. This will cause severe difficulties for companies which had written policies against such risks. This is likely to be the largest insurance payout the world has ever seen. Lloyds of London alone is expected to face a bill of $9 billion (partly offset by the practice of re-insurance, whereby Lloyds has off-loaded some of its risks to other insurance companies). Lloyds' net liability is thought to be around $2 billion. Long-term, the prospects are for higher insurance premiums wherever a terrorist threat can be identified. Already airlines, airports and major events, such as the 2002 World Cup Final, have been hit by a huge escalation in premiums.

TOURISM: The continuing crisis is very damaging for the tourism industry, which relies upon confidence in travel and the safety of destinations. Both have been affected. Tourist destinations such as Central London have been hard hit. This is normally a very popular destination for American tourists, but in the autumn of 2001 bookings from the USA slumped. Hotels, restaurants, conference centres and visitor attractions are all affected. Even car hire companies such as Hertz, Avis and Europcar have suffered, with business at UK airports down 60% in the early aftermath of September 11.

BUSINESS AND CONSUMER CONFIDENCE

Direct effects, such as the closure of New York as a financial sector for five days, followed by the quantifiable effects on the industries mentioned above, dominated the news headlines in the weeks after the terrorist attack. However, it is the longer term effect on business and consumer confidence in the USA and other leading economies which will matter most for the global economy. Early indications were not good. Survey data collected shortly after the terrorist attacks showed, understandably, that consumer confidence had been shattered, accelerating a downward trend which was already noticeable.

Further data, released in October, showed a savage drop in US orders for durable goods. This is a mix of longer lasting consumer items such as washing machines, refrigerators and cars, plus business expenditure on aircraft, computers, electronics and communications equipment. In one month aircraft orders plunged by 29%, and communications equipment by 39%. Overall, durable goods orders were down 13% compared to October 2000.

A cause for cautious optimism, however, is that consumer confidence quickly rebounded on both sides of the Atlantic. This occurred against all 'expert' predictions, and robust consumer spending prevented the recession turning into the economic slump which might have been expected.

INTERNATIONAL POLICY RESPONSES

Economic policy makers can try to offset the global effect of major economic shocks, such as the terrorists attacks, by taking prompt corrective action:

INTEREST RATES: Interest rates in the USA, Britain and Europe have been reduced in the wake of September 11, and liquidity pumped into the global banking system to try to avert financial collapse. Ordinary businesses have received a boost because consumers have been encouraged by low interest rates to borrow and spend. Lower interest rates also tend to make equity shares more attractive to hold because they reduce the return on investments in bonds and bank deposits. This was desperately needed when the US financial markets reopened five days after the attack. The world's investors held their breath. After initial declines of just under 20%, equity markets responded to interest rate cuts and reassuring words of encouragement from leading bankers, to recover most of their lost ground. In the short term the policy had worked, but share prices remained vulnerable to further declines in the world economy and nervousness about the risk of further terrorist attacks.

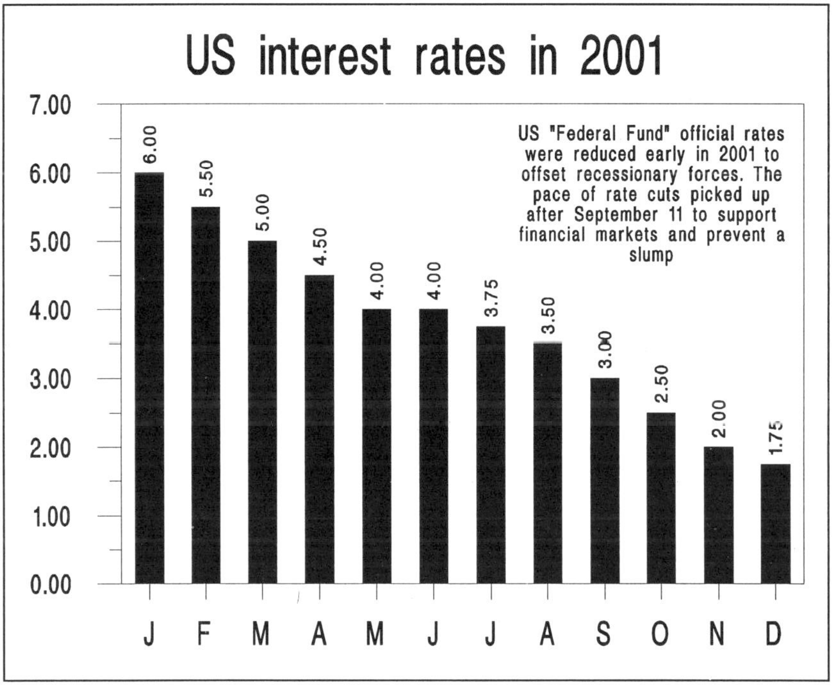

FISCAL POLICY: President Bush had already begun to plan serious tax cuts before September 2001. Add in the additional military expenditure, government aid to the airline industry, emergency help for New York, and the costs of heightened security, and the US economy is likely to experience a $150 billion fiscal boost which will go some way towards offsetting the recessionary effects of the War against Terrorism.

BUSINESS BRIEFING: WORLD RECESSION

World recession can affect individual businesses in many ways.

EXPORTS: Export orders tend to dry up, particularly to those economies which are worst affected.

COMPETITION: Competition to maintain market share becomes intense, with discounting and other promotions needed in markets at home and abroad.

PROFITS: Profits are squeezed by reduced sales and difficulties in reducing fixed costs in the short term.

CONFIDENCE: Confidence is eroded by recession and this can lead businesses to shelve their investment and expansion programmes. Businesses which wish to press ahead with investments may face difficulties in raising finance if lenders become risk averse.

UK ECONOMIC GROWTH

Concerns over a global slowdown have caused economists in the UK to keep a particularly close watch over the rate of economic growth. However, during 2001 there was little sign that the recessionary forces seen in other countries had been mirrored in the UK. Overall, the rate of growth of GDP has been tracking only slightly below the long term national average of around 2.5%.

The Gross Domestic Product (GDP) measures the output of the whole UK economy. The figures shown in the chart are the increase in GDP each quarter compared to one year earlier after the effects of inflation have been removed. This is the most commonly used measure of economic growth.

The chart clearly shows the path of the last UK recession in 1991/92, with negative growth rates indicating a contraction of economic activity. Since the end of the recession the GDP has risen for thirty-seven successive quarters - over nine years of growth. This is a post-war record, with the previous longest expansion being between 1984 and 1990.

Growth rates have fluctuated from year to year since 1992, but the economy has been much more stable than it was in the 1980s, when the decade started with a major recession and ended with an unsustainable "boom" which turned to "bust" during 1990.

Steady economic growth is helpful for a lot of people:

- Businesses can concentrate on winning market share rather than worrying that demand is about to collapse.
- Individuals are likely to find jobs more plentiful during periods of economic growth. In a recession unemployment usually rises as employers shed labour to cut costs.

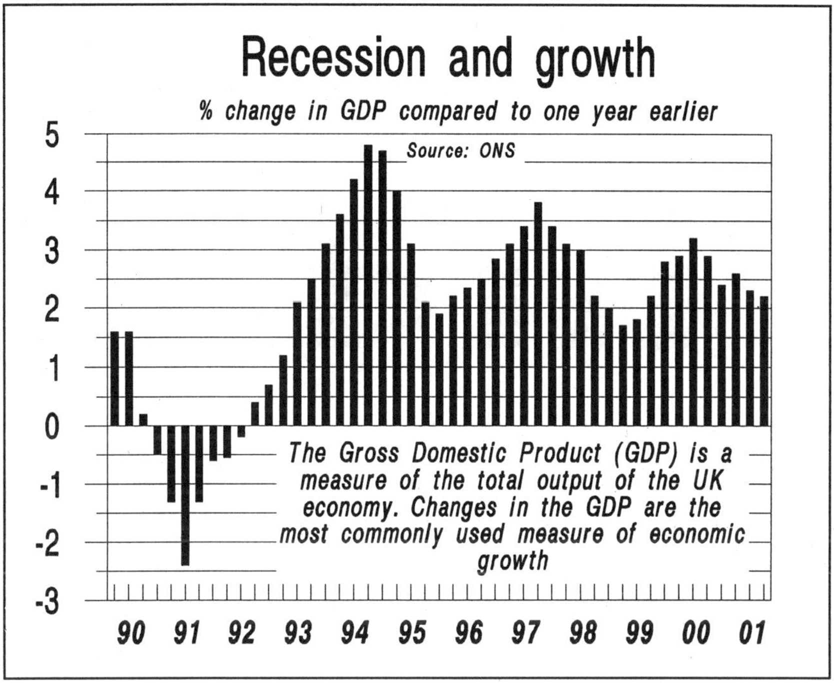

* The government benefits because it collects steadily increasing amounts of tax which can be ploughed into the public services.

ECONOMIC SECTORS

Whilst the UK economy as a whole has enjoyed remarkable growth and stability in recent times, the same cannot be said for individual economic sectors.

AGRICULTURE: The figures shown in the graph on the next page actually relate to production in agriculture, hunting, forestry and fishing. Fishing has been subject to steady long term decline because of dwindling fish stocks and EU quota restrictions. Hunting and forestry are relatively minor components. The hefty falls in production in 2000 and 2001 are mainly due to the well-publicised misfortunes of agriculture.

During 2001 the main problems faced by farmers were caused by the disastrous Foot and Mouth crisis, which led to the slaughter of millions of sheep and cattle and costly disruption to the livestock sector as a whole. The worst affected areas were Cumbria, Dumfries and Galloway, Devon, Wales, Northumberland and Yorkshire. In addition to farmers who lost their stock through culling, many farmers in those areas were not able to take their produce to market because of movement restrictions to contain the disease. Exports of animals and meat products were temporarily banned due to the

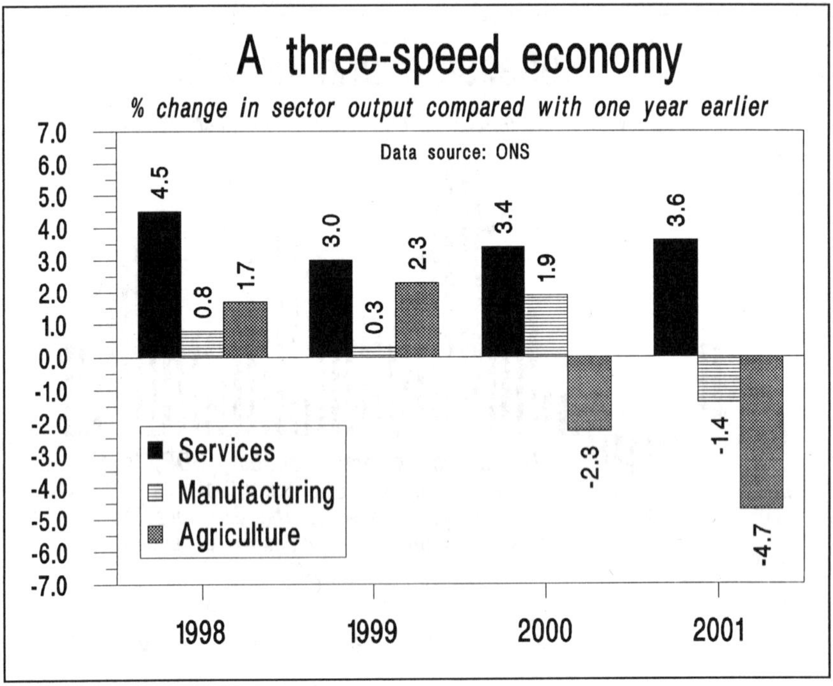

risks of spreading the infection. Coming on top of the earlier BSE crisis and depressed international markets for farm products, UK agriculture has been experiencing its worst period of decline for decades.

The rural economy more generally has suffered from Foot and Mouth, particularly through the loss of revenues from tourism. Hotels, pubs, restaurants, retailers and visitor attractions in affected areas suffered dramatic falls in business as people stayed away. Of course, some of this business, which shows up in the statistics for the service sectors, was simply redirected to city and coastal tourism, so the impact on the economy as a whole has been muted. There is little doubt, however, that specific local economies, such as the Lake District, Devon and parts of North Yorkshire, suffered sharp recessions.

MANUFACTURING: Britain's factories also had a bad year in 2001. Hi-tech industries, such as computers, office equipment and telecommunications manufacturing, led the downturn in a reversal of an earlier boom in production.

The manufacture of motor vehicles and consumer goods for the UK market remained quite strong. Food and pharmaceutical manufacturers also maintained output and orders.

After September 11 orders for civilian aircraft slumped, with severe implications for aerospace manufacturers such as BAE Systems.

Manufacturing is one of the sectors most exposed to the effects of deteriorating global economic conditions. Recession in other countries, such as the USA, Japan and Germany, leads to loss of UK exports to those markets. The lack of global demand for manufactured goods also tends to encourage cut-throat competition and price cuts which damage profitability.

The downturn in UK manufacturing in 2001 has started to have a serious impact on employment. The number of jobs in this sector fell by 141,000 from October 2000 to October 2001, reducing the total manufacturing workforce to 3,792,000.

The British Chambers of Commerce (BCC) say that manufacturing needs intensive care, and whilst the Bank of England's cuts in interest rates offered the right kind of medicine, they may not be enough to bring the sector back to health. BCC director general, David Lennan, says ***These are tough and uncertain times for the UK and global economy and all the indicators point to the fact that there is worse to come.***

Manufacturing trends in the UK are beginning to mirror those in the USA, where industry has undergone its longest recession for over fifty years. Even before the September attacks on the USA, twelve successive monthly declines in US manufacturing production had been reported - the longest since 1945.

SERVICES: Growth in the UK economy as a whole has been supported by a buoyant service sector. Services are by far the largest sector of the economy and have been set on a course of long term expansion. Over 22 million people are employed in services. A vast array of activities are included in services. These include:

- Distribution, hotels, catering and repairs
- Transport, storage and communications
- Business services and finance
- Other services.

During the year to June 2001 each of these sub-sectors showed brisk rates of expansion.

Large parts of the public sector also fall within the definition of the service sector. Due to recent increases in government expenditure, services such as health and education are expanding and recruiting additional staff.

Towards the end of 2001 concerns were voiced from a number of quarters that economic weakness, evident in manufacturing and agriculture, was also spreading to services. In July a survey by the BCC suggested that companies selling business services to manufacturers were beginning to suffer. The Foot and Mouth epidemic was also damaging tourism related services.

After September 11, real distress was felt in the airline industry and in London-based tourism. There was also a sharp drop in confidence that other parts of the service sector would be able to maintain their health. Newspaper financial columns were full of despair. Analysts speculated that consumers would curb their spending, particularly on luxury items, and the leisure industry would be hit by cancelled events due to security concerns, conferences and exhibitions postponed and tourists staying at home.

The Chartered Institute of Purchasing and Supply appeared, in its November survey, to reinforce these fears, reporting a sharp contraction in service activity. In the short term, however, these alarming claims seem to have been overdone, with little hard evidence emerging to show that concerns expressed in surveys had been translated into overall decline in the service sector. Indeed, important elements, such as retailing, showed unexpected buoyancy towards the end of 2001.

The service sector will be closely monitored during 2002 for any sign of weakness, since the economy's ability to avoid overall recession largely depends on continued growth of services to offset contraction elsewhere.

CONSUMER BEHAVIOUR

One of the greatest threats to continued economic growth in the UK would be a severe cutback in consumer spending. Gloomy talk about recession, global economic crises and war against international terrorists could easily damage consumers' confidence and cause them to economise, defer large purchases, and stay at home instead of travelling or visiting the shopping mall. In a modern economy, such a reaction on a widespread scale would damage growth. Particularly when export markets are contracting, the last thing our businesses need is a reduction in UK consumer expenditure. No wonder, in the aftermath of September 11, Prime Minister Tony Blair urged Britons ***to work, to live, to travel and to shop*** exactly as they had done before.

The Bank of England also played its part by reducing interest rates, which reduces the cost of consumer credit. Even so, economists and business analysts have watched with unusual concern the regular flow of data on consumer trends - in particular retail expenditure.

AVERAGE WEEKLY EXPENDITURE BY HOUSEHOLDS IN THE UK IN 2000-01

	£
Leisure goods and services	70.40
Housing	63.90
Food and non-alcoholic drink	61.90
Motoring	55.10
Household goods and services	54.60
Clothing and footwear	22.00
Alcoholic drink	15.00
Personal goods and services	14.70
Fuel and power	11.90
Fares and other travel costs	9.50
Tobacco	6.10
Miscellaneous	0.70
Total expenditure	**385.70**

Source: Family Expenditure Survey, Office of National Statistics

RETAIL SALES

Remarkably, retail sales, one of the key indicators of household consumption, has remained extremely buoyant in spite of otherwise gloomy economic news. In fact, it is largely down to plucky consumers that the UK is not immediately following the USA and other economies into recession.

HOUSEHOLD DEBT

Consumers, during 2001, largely financed their additional expenditure by borrowing. Household disposable income, which had been rising steadily in 1999 and 2000, shrank back in 2001 because of higher tax payments. Instead of spending less to reflect this reduction in incomes, however, households took advantage of low interest rates on various forms of credit to spend even more.

In the short run, this ***buy now - pay later*** attitude has helped the economy stay buoyant, but there are longer term risks:

* Record levels of household debt may be affordable whilst interest rates stay low, but could lead to repayment difficulties if they rise. Interest rates in 2001 have been at their lowest level for decades, but could increase again at any time.

* If the economy continues to slow, or does go into recession, some households might face the dual problem of unemployment and indebtedness.

* Rising house prices have encouraged some households to borrow additional sums against the value of their homes. This is sometimes referred to as ***equity withdrawal*** - a process by which home owners cash in on the surplus value of their property over and above any mortgage debt they owe. In one month alone, October 2001, over 57,000 borrowers extended existing home loans, raising £1.1 billion through equity withdrawal. This money will have been spent on retail items, home improvements, holidays and cars.

  For some borrowers this could end in tears. The loans taken out are secured on the value of their home, and failure to make repayments could cause their bank or building society to repossess the property.

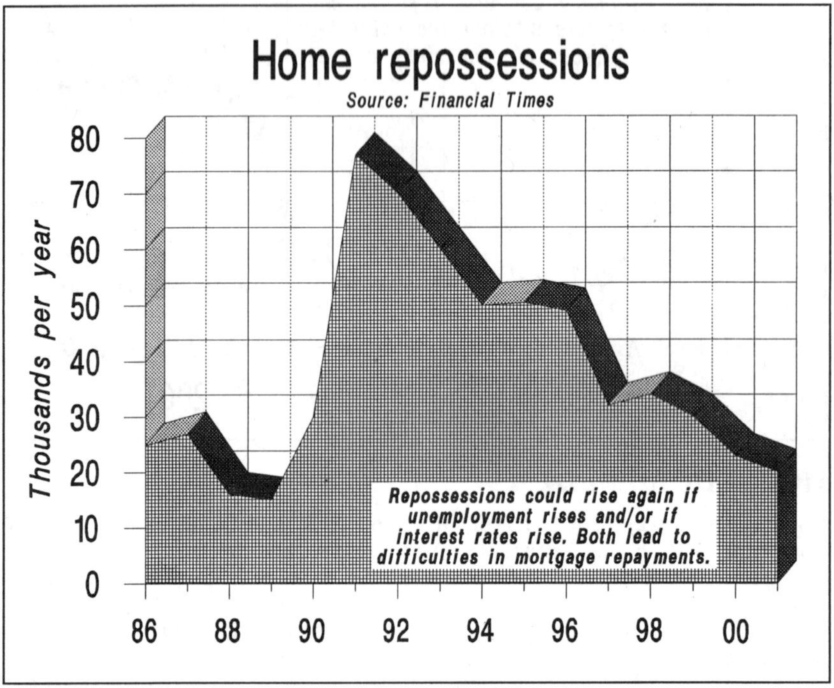

Repossessions soared in the early 1990s in similar circumstances. The consumption and house price boom of the late 1980s had caused a huge increase in mortgage debt. When interest rates soared in 1990/91, nearly 80,000 families lost their homes in a single year due to failure to make repayments, and subsequent repossessions.

Further evidence that the credit-financed spending boom is unsustainable comes from the Bank of England data on household debt. This shows that the total value of mortgage debt and consumer credit has soared to a record level of 70% of GDP. At the height of the last consumer boom in 1988, the comparable ratio was 50%. This situation has caused Sir Howard Davies, head of the Financial Services Authority, to warn that consumer borrowing is excessive. Also the Office of Fair Trading has launched a ***Keep Debt Under Control*** campaign, with the slogan ***Think before you borrow.***

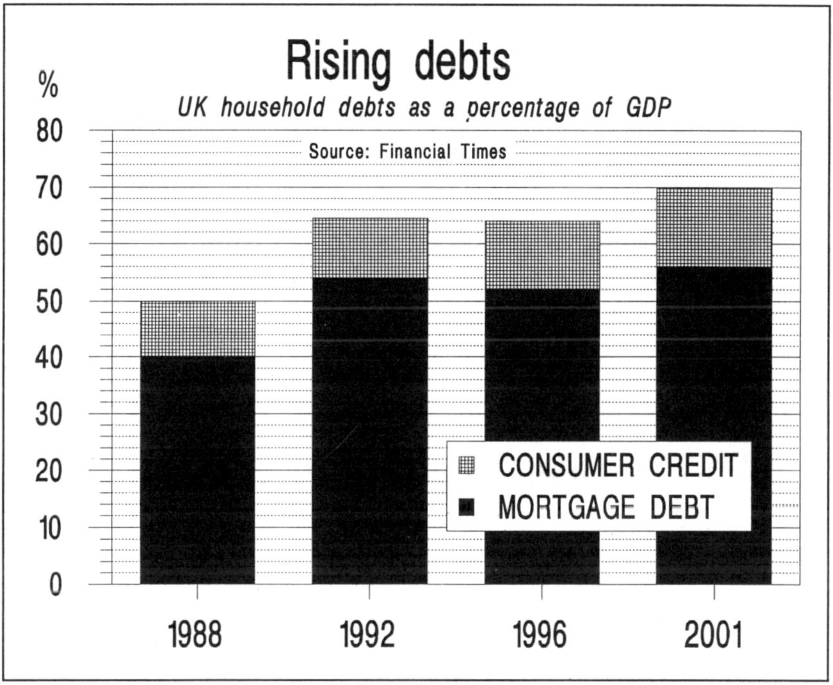

UNEMPLOYMENT

The long period of economic expansion from 1992 onwards has corresponded with a dramatic reduction in unemployment. Low unemployment is good for the economy in a number of respects:

- People find it easier to find work, boosting household incomes.
- Businesses benefit from buoyant consumer markets.
- The government's finances improve because more people pay income tax and fewer claim unemployment benefits.

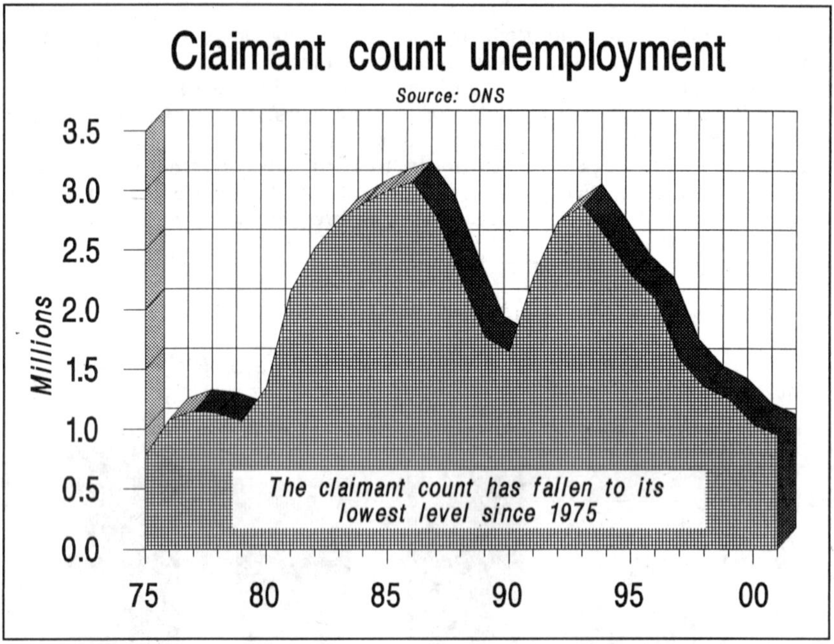
Claimant count unemployment
Source: ONS
3.5
3.0
2.5
2.0
1.5
1.0
0.5
0.0
Millions
The claimant count has fallen to its lowest level since 1975
75
80
85
90
95
00

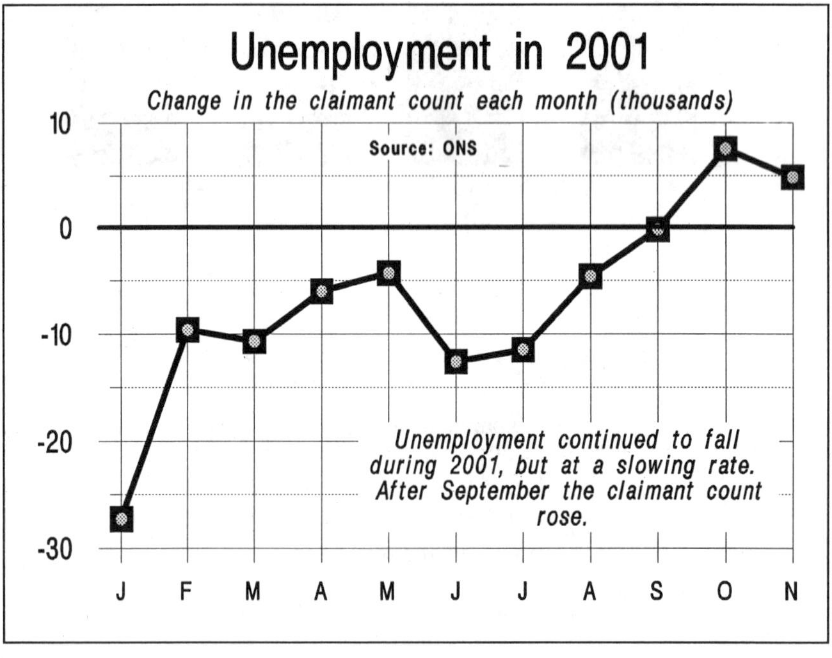
Unemployment in 2001
Change in the claimant count each month (thousands)
Source: ONS
10
0
-10
-20
-30
Unemployment continued to fall during 2001, but at a slowing rate. After September the claimant count rose.
J
F
M
A
M
J
J
A
S
O
N

The claimant count is the oldest established method of measuring unemployment. It is based on the claims made by unemployed people for benefits, including the Job Seeker's Allowance.

Whilst the long term unemployment trend has been downwards, there are some signs that this is coming to an end, with rising unemployment towards the end of 2001. The lowest point appears to have been reached in September, when claimant count unemployment stood at 946,800, or 3.1% of the workforce.

The previous graph shows monthly fluctuations in the claimant count, and this gives a very detailed insight into small changes in the number of people claiming benefits. Readers should continue to monitor this trend in 2002. Monthly unemployment statistics are well publicised in the press. A substantial rise in unemployment would be a good indicator that the UK economy was beginning to succumb to the forces of global recession.

LABOUR FORCE SURVEY

The reliability of the claimant count as an accurate measure of unemployment has been questioned on many occasions. It is generally regarded as an under-estimate of true unemployment, because some people are out of work but cannot, or do not chose to, register for unemployment related benefits. In recent years a second measure of unemployment has been introduced, based on the Labour Force Survey (LFS).

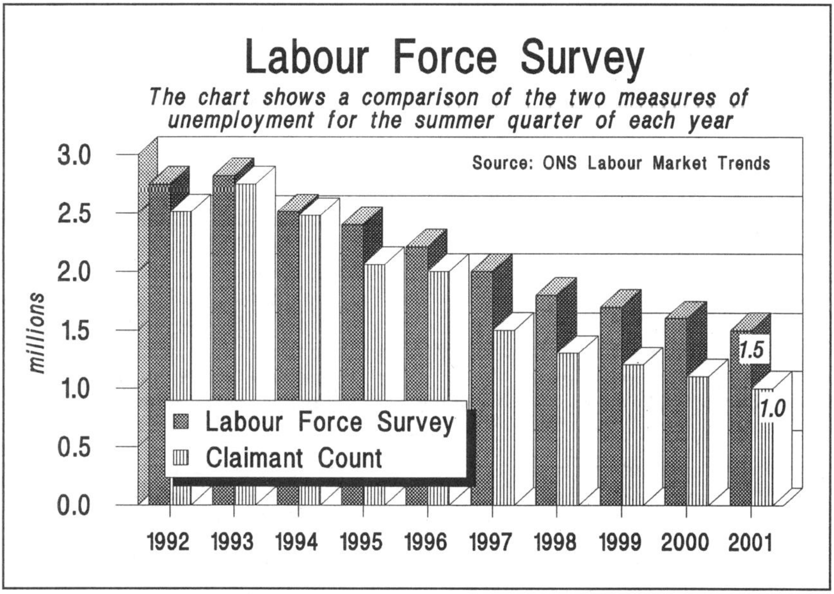

The LFS is the biggest regular household survey in Britain, covering approximately 150,000 people each quarter. It counts as unemployed:

- Those who were without a job at the time the survey was conducted ***and*** who
- were available to start work in the next fortnight ***and***
- had actively looked for work in the last four weeks ***or***
- had found a job and were waiting to start.

The LFS confirms the long run downward trend in unemployment, but shows a slower pace of decline. The LFS indicates that the ***true*** rate of unemployment in summer 2001 was approximately 5.1%, or 1.5 million people out of work.

INFLATION

During 2001 the headline rate of inflation, measured by the annual change in the Retail Prices Index (RPI), fell below 1% for the first time in thirty-eight years.

The headline rate of inflation is widely used in wage bargaining as the accepted measure of changes in the cost of living. It fell sharply in November 2001 to just 0.9%, mainly due to lower petrol prices and other fuel costs.

RPIX v Headline Inflation

Policy makers prefer to use RPIX (underlying inflation, which excludes the effects of mortgage interest payments) rather than RPI (headline inflation). For years it was always inflation measured by changes in the RPI which made the news headlines. The problem with this was the distorting effects which changes in interest rates could have on the RPI.

In recent years, increasing use has been made of interest rate changes to control inflation. A forecast is made eighteen months to two years ahead, predicting the likely rate of inflation. If this is above the target, the Bank of England is likely to raise its base rate, which in turn leads to a more general increase in interest rates in the private sector at commercial banks, building societies and credit card companies, etc. This has proved to be very effective in controlling inflation in the medium term, but the short term effect is usually to ***increase*** headline inflation because the RPI includes mortgage costs. This responsiveness to base rate changes has tended to make RPI a less reliable and more volatile measure of inflation, as can be seen in the graph on the next page.

Success in keeping underlying inflation close to the government's target rate of 2.5% allowed the Bank of England to cut interest rates sharply during 2001. This is explained further in the feature on INTEREST RATES.

The scale of this success is best judged against the UK's own past performance. Inflation used to be a major problem, particularly in the mid 1970s when the underlying rate peaked at 28%.

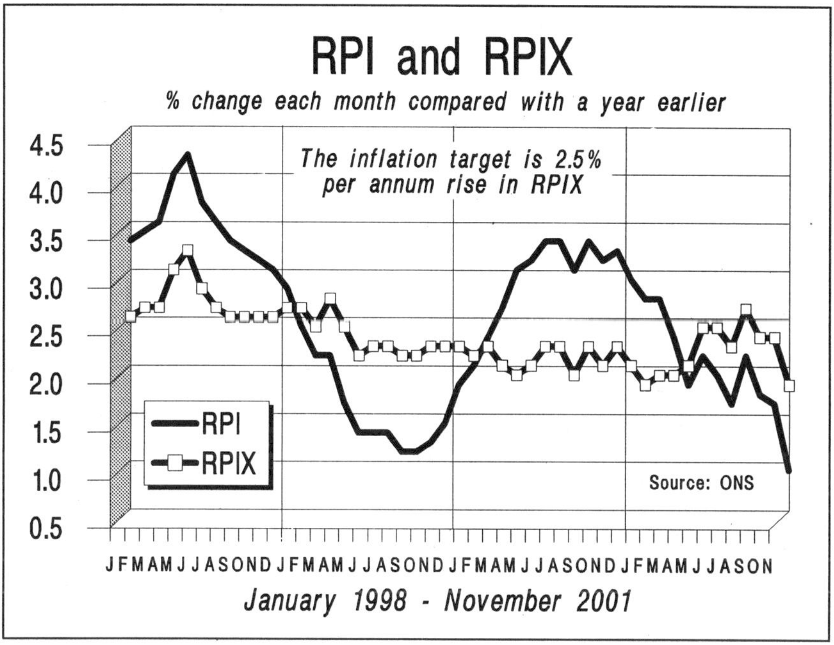
RPI and RPIX
% change each month compared with a year earlier
The inflation target is 2.5% per annum rise in RPIX
4.5
4.0
3.5
3.0
2.5
2.0
1.5
1.0
0.5
RPI
RPIX
Source: ONS
J F M A M J J A S O N D J F M A M J J A S O N D J F M A M J J A S O N D J F M A M J J A S O N
January 1998 - November 2001

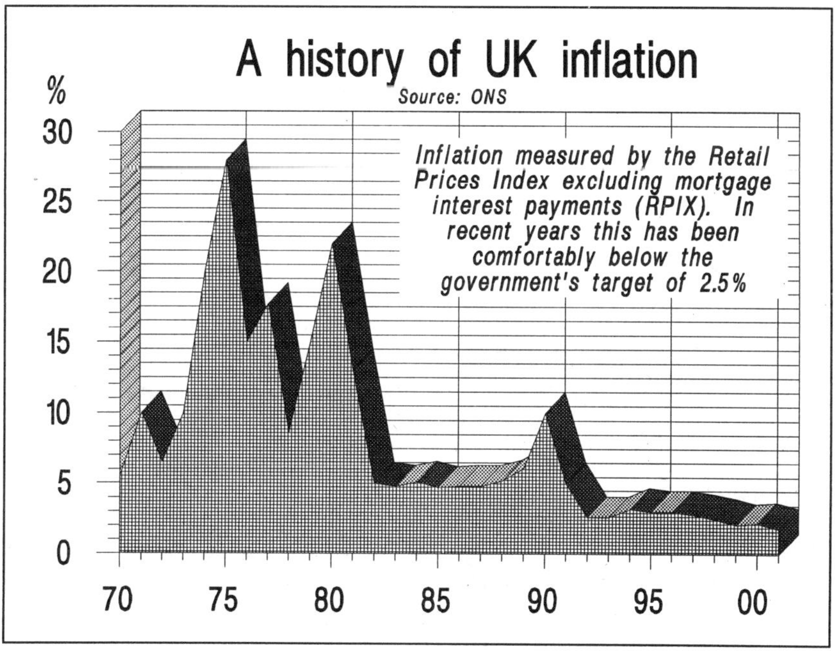
A history of UK inflation
Source: ONS
%
30
25
20
15
10
5
0
Inflation measured by the Retail Prices Index excluding mortgage interest payments (RPIX). In recent years this has been comfortably below the government's target of 2.5%
70
75
80
85
90
95
00

INFLATION FACT FILE

Annual percentage change, November 2000 to November 2001

Raw materials and fuel prices	-11.1
Factory gate prices	-1.0
Retail prices (headline)	+0.9
Retail prices (underlying)	+1.8
Average earnings	+4.4

Source: Sunday Times Databank

BALANCE OF PAYMENTS

The UK's balance of payments current account continues to show a substantial deficit. The current account is predominantly made up of the trade in goods and services;

TRADE IN GOODS: This involves the ***visible*** elements of overseas trade, such as food, basic raw materials, oil, other fuels, and manufactured goods. Historically Britain earned surpluses in this category, but since the mid 1980s the decline in our industrial base has meant that large deficits have become a familiar pattern.

TRADE IN SERVICES: Trade in services is sometimes referred to as ***invisibles***. This category includes financial services, insurance, computer and information services, travel and transportation, etc. Surpluses are regularly recorded.

The current account also includes net income from overseas investments and the foreign earnings of employees, plus current transfers between the UK and overseas governments and other institutions. However, these are of lesser significance than the value of trade in goods and services.

During 2000 the UK current account was in overall deficit by £14 billion. A similar deficit is expected in 2001, after which the government forecasts a deterioration to around £25 billion. This is mainly due to the adverse outlook for UK exports in a period of global recession.

As the graph on the next page shows, the UK is used to coping with a current account deficit. As a percentage of GDP, the deficits of the late 1980s were much greater than anything witnessed in recent years. The deterioration in the current account would have to be severe before it began to threaten UK growth and economic stability.

The impact of a slowing global economy is mainly felt by the UK's industrial sector and shows up in the visible trade statistics referred to as the ***global trade balance.*** This is falling into increasing deficit as exports to depressed overseas markets falter, whilst imports continue to be sucked into the UK by the boom in consumer spending.

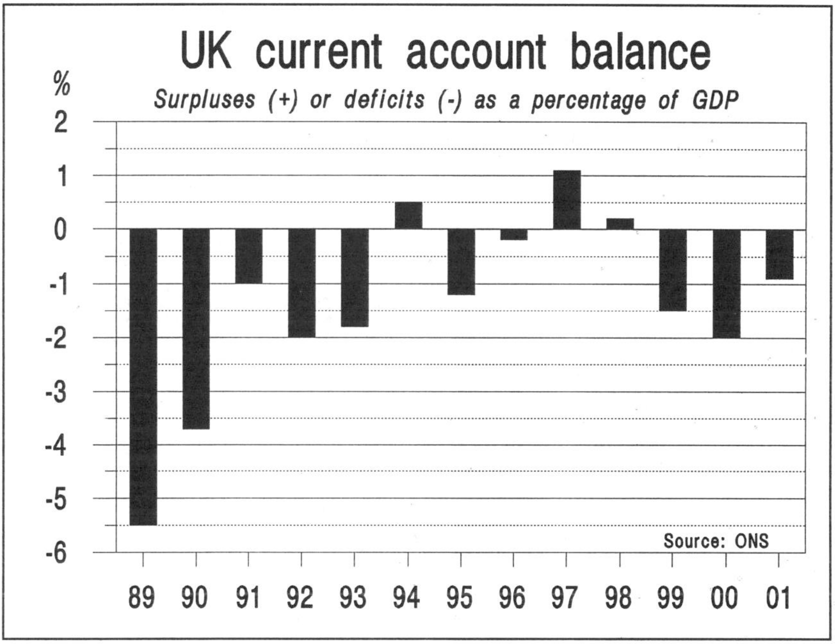
UK current account balance
Surpluses (+) or deficits (-) as a percentage of GDP
%
2
1
0
-1
-2
-3
-4
-5
-6
Source: ONS
89
90
91
92
93
94
95
96
97
98
99
00
01

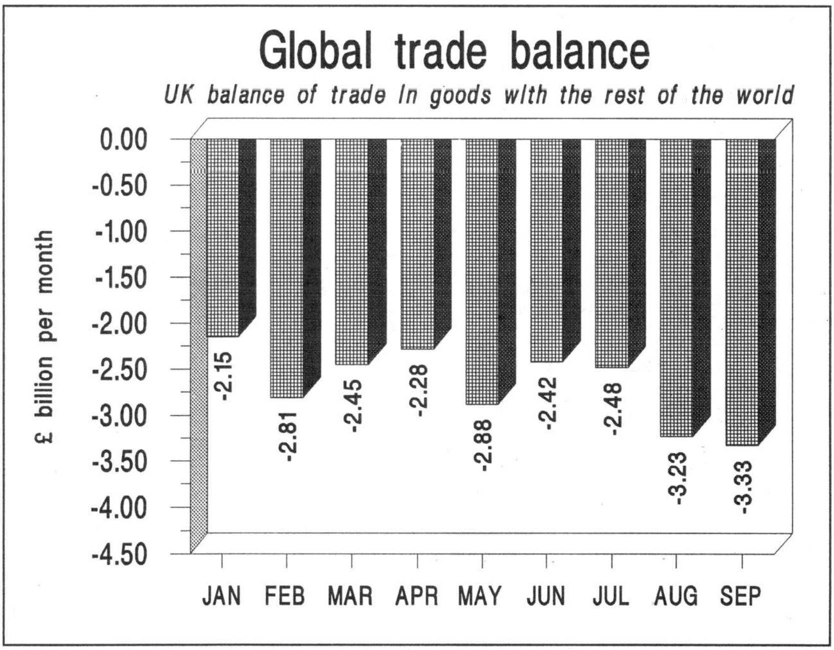
Global trade balance
UK balance of trade in goods with the rest of the world
£ billion per month
0.00
-0.50
-1.00
-1.50
-2.00
-2.50
-3.00
-3.50
-4.00
-4.50
-2.15
-2.81
-2.45
-2.28
-2.88
-2.42
-2.48
-3.23
-3.33
JAN
FEB
MAR
APR
MAY
JUN
JUL
AUG
SEP

EXCHANGE RATES

A further factor which has made international trade difficult for UK manufacturers is the strength of the pound sterling against other currencies.

The sterling ***trade weighted index*** shows a composite value of the pound against a basket of other currencies according to their individual importance in UK overseas trade. It is the best single measure of the strength of the pound on foreign exchange markets.

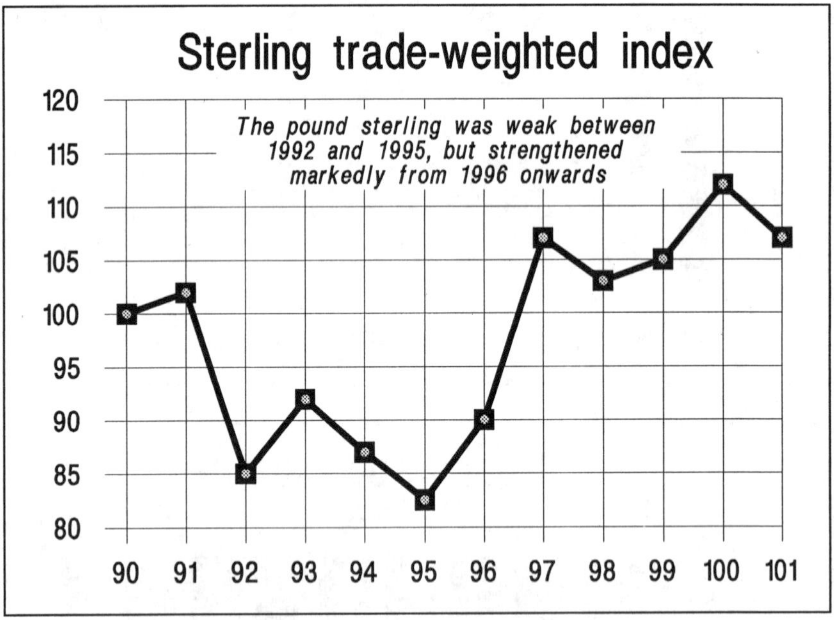

The sterling index is based on 1990 = 100. In 1992 the pound was effectively devalued as it crashed out of the European Exchange Rate Mechanism (ERM). Between 1992 and 1996 exporters enjoyed a competitive advantage over their foreign rivals because a low exchange rate makes British goods appear relatively cheap when expressed in other currencies. A sterling index value of 85, for example, represents a 15% depreciation compared with 1990 levels. Since 1996 the pound has strengthened and this has reversed the advantages for exporters. Industry has faced intense pressure to cut costs in order to remain competitive. Profit margins have also suffered as many businesses have tried to absorb the effects of the rising pound and maintain competitive prices on foreign markets.

A strong pound does have advantages, however, for some. It has made consumers feel better off because their incomes stretch further on imported goods and the things they buy on holiday overseas. This has undoubtedly strengthened the ***feel good*** factor which has pervaded the UK population in recent times.

INTEREST RATES

Interest rates are one of the main monetary tools available to control the economy. During 2001 the Bank of England's base rate fell to 4%, its lowest level for thirty-eight years. The reduction in this key interest rate indicator from 6.0% at the beginning of the year reflects concerns that the British economy might be heading for a period of very slow growth (or recession) with unusually low rates of inflation.

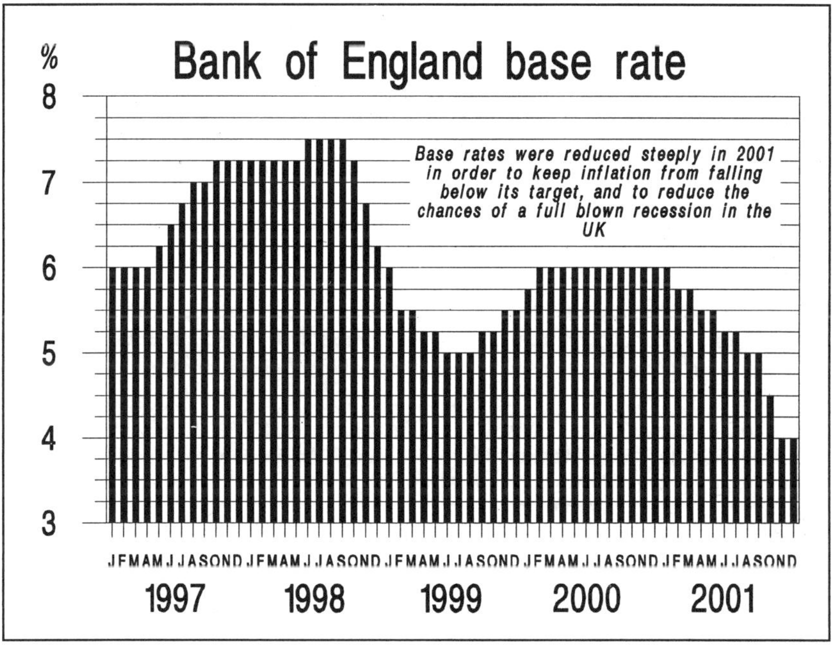

Monetary policy, principally through the control of Bank of England base rate, has been the main policy instrument used in recent years to control inflation and maintain price stability. For example, inflation worries in 1997/8 were met with increases in base rate, peaking at 7.5%. Once the outlook for inflation improved, base rate was sharply reduced through 1998/9 in order to stimulate growth and prevent recession from taking hold. The economy rebounded strongly in 1999, and rising wages and salaries plus a modest boom in house prices turned the Bank of England's attention once again to price stability. Base rates were driven upwards again, but this time they peaked at only 6.00%.

Base rate increases have a favourable effect on inflation through:

1. Increasing the cost of borrowing and so discouraging the demand for credit to finance purchases of consumer goods and investment goods.

2. Reducing the demand for consumer goods by further increasing mortgage rates and squeezing real incomes.
3. Pushing up the exchange rate for the pound against foreign currencies. This reduces inflation through a downward effect on import prices, and also puts British manufacturers under pressure to cut costs to stay competitive.

Reduced interest rates have the opposite effects. The demand for credit is boosted, mortgage rates fall, and the pressure on manufacturers is reduced. Businesses, as well as consumers, can cope with any debts they have run up more easily because lower interest rates means lower repayments. Base rates are generally reduced in this way only when there is considered to be an absence of inflationary forces in the economy. The full effects of base rate changes take effect after eighteen to twenty-four months as businesses and consumers gradually adjust their investment and spending patterns.

THE INFLATION TARGET: When the Labour government took power in 1997, one of its first acts was to put the control of inflation firmly in the hands of the Bank of England, which was given operational independence. The Bank of England does, however, have an inflation ***target*** set by the government, of 2.5%, and must try to keep inflation within 1% above or below this figure.

As shown earlier, underlying inflation has tracked considerably below the government's target throughout 2001. The Bank of England has taken the view that interest rates needed to fall to keep inflation above 1.5% in the foreseeable future.

If the inflation rate falls below 1.5% (or rises above 3.5%) the Governor of the Bank of England is required by law to write to the Chancellor of the Exchequer to explain why. It is a measure of the Bank's success since 1997 that he has never needed to do this. However, some economists argue that inflation will fall so low in 2002 that the Governor will have to write such a letter for the first time.

FISCAL POLICY

Fiscal policy, the setting of tax rates and public expenditure levels, is one of the most important aspects of the government's management of the economy. It is the responsibility of the Chancellor of the Exchequer, assisted by his civil service department, the Treasury.

There are two set piece events in the parliamentary calendar through which fiscal policy is carried out:

1. The Budget - in March
2. The Pre-Budget Report - in November of each year, which allows the Chancellor to set out his plans for the following year.

BUDGET 2001

This was the last Budget before the general election, and it gave the Chancellor the opportunity to show how successfully he was managing the economy. In the early years of the Labour government (elected in 1997) Gordon Brown had earned his reputation as ***the Iron Chancellor*** - a tough controller of the public finances who had imposed "fiscal discipline" over his government colleagues.

The Labour Party used to have a reputation for reckless public expenditure policies which led to economic crises. In order to become electable, the present Labour government had to promise not to spend excessively. In fact, they guaranteed to stick to previously published Conservative public expenditure targets for the first two years of their term of office (1997-98 and 1998-99). Combined with the growth of the economy, which has generated higher than expected tax receipts, this fiscal prudence has led to large budget surpluses. This gave the Chancellor the scope in his crucial pre-election Budget to cut taxes, increase public expenditure and repay debt.

The strength of the public finances allowed the Chancellor to display apparent generosity to families (maternity pay increased); to the elderly (state pension raised by £5 a week); to children (extra funding to improve schools and recruit teachers); and to the sick (through extra spending on the NHS).

Repaying debt

Gordon Brown is proud of his record in repaying public debt. He has set a rule by which the debt to GDP ratio must be kept below 40%. In 2001 it was 31.8%. Falling debt (and lower interest rates) has dramatically reduced the costs of servicing past government extravagence. Mr Brown, when delivering his Budget speech, said ***In 1997 Britain spent more on debt interest payments than all the money it spent on schools. In 2001/2 we will be spending £10 billion a year more on schools than on debt interest charges.*** Reduced unemployment has also saved £4 billion a year from social security costs since 1997 - money now available for frontline public services.

Cutting taxes

Having ***raised*** taxes in earlier Budgets, Gordon Brown was now in a position to appear generous and return money to the taxpayer:

- Working families tax credit - up £5 per week
- Children's tax credit - up from £8.50 to £10.00
- The lowest 10 pence income tax band was increased from the first £1,520 of taxable income to £1,880

These measures were particularly designed to help the less well off. Cuts in petrol and road vehicle taxes, worth a total of £2 billion a year, were also introduced in order to avoid a repeat performance of the fuel tax protests of the previous year.

GOVERNMENT INCOME AND EXPENDITURE 2001/02

Income (£ bn)		Expenditure (£ bn)	
Income tax	104	Social Security	109
VAT	61	NHS	59
National Insurance	63	Education	50
Excise duties	37	Debt interest	23
Corporation tax	38	Defence	24
Business rates	17	Law and order	23
Council tax	15	Industry, agriculture	
Other	64	and employment	16
		Housing and environment	18
		Transport	10
		Other expenditure	62
Total	**398**	**Total**	**394**

Public Sector Debt Repayment (PSDR) = £4 billion

Raising spending

Economics Update 2001 reported on the government's Comprehensive Spending Review, which injected £43 billion into public services over the period 2001/2004. By comparison, the 2001 Budget looked like small scale tinkering. Previously announced intentions to raise public expenditure by 3.4% per annum for three years were increased to 3.7%.

2001 PRE-BUDGET REPORT

By the time of the 27 November Pre-Budget Report, concerns over the health of the world economy had become more serious. Although the Chancellor was able to say that he expected the UK to cope with the global slowdown more easily than most other major economies, he was still forced to concede that the overall budget would soon return to deficit.

By comparison with past performance, the projected deficit is quite manageable. It is much lower as a percentage of GDP than the deficit "inherited" from the Conservative government in 1997. The reliability of these projections depends much upon the ability of the UK to avoid recession. If growth, assumed to be 2% - 2.5% in the Pre-Budget Report, turns out to be much lower, the deficit could soar. This is because slower growth results in:

- Reduced tax revenues from income tax, corporation tax, VAT, etc.
- Increased public expenditure on social security payments as unemployment rises.

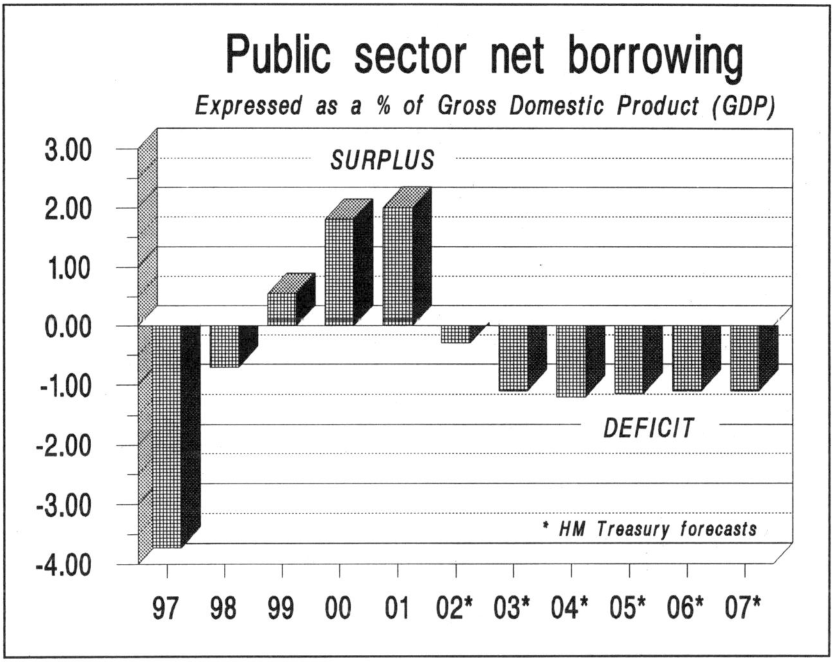

National Health Service

In a major shift in government policy, the Chancellor has committed himself to a long term increase in the share of GDP to be spent on the NHS - the top priority in public service improvements demanded by many voters.

The government has promised not to raise the basic or top rates of income tax during the rest of the current parliament, but there are plenty of ways of increasing tax revenue to pay for an improved health service. National Insurance payments by workers and their employers could be increased, VAT could rise, or extra tax could be applied to a host of goods and services such as alcohol and tobacco.

OIL SUPPLIES

In our feature on ***The World Economy*** we saw that periods of international tension are often associated with volatile oil prices. This can clearly be seen in the chart on the next page.

Oil prices are very sensitive to the forces of supply and demand.

WAR: Major disruption to oil supplies, such as war in the Middle East, can cause oil prices to suddenly rise. This was very evident in the 1970s.

SPECULATION: Sudden movements in the price of oil are also caused by speculators. Oil is a major world commodity, and when a shortage is predicted speculators try to buy up existing oil stocks so they can sell at a profit later. In 1990, for example, it was mainly the speculators who drove up the price of oil after Iraq invaded Kuwait. In the event, oil supplies were hardly affected by this particular conflict because other oil producers (particularly Saudi Arabia) were able to increase production to compensate for lost supplies from Iraq and Kuwait. Once commodity dealers realised this, speculative buying of oil ceased and the world price sank back below $20 a barrel very quickly.

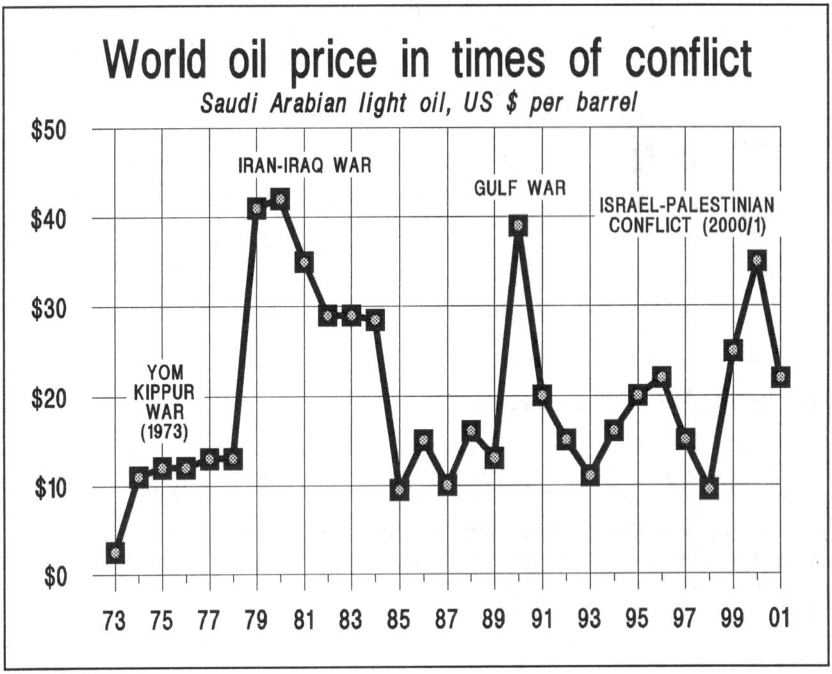

SEPTEMBER 11: Once again, as at the outset of the Gulf War, oil prices soared to nearly $30 a barrel as dealers feared that supplies would be interrupted. Once it became clear that most oil producing countries had sided with the USA, the price fell back to levels lower than they had stood at before September 11. This is because the world price of oil is affected by forces of demand as well as supply. The fall in the oil price was caused by a commonly held view that supply would not be affected, but demand would decline as so many countries were heading for recession and associated declines in industrial production.

A low oil price is helpful in stabilising the world economy, but some economists argue that it is foolish for America and other industrial economies to be so dependent on supplies from the turbulent Middle East. One country alone, Saudi Arabia, controls 12% of world production and 25% of known oil reserves. Saudi Arabia has been friendly to the West for many years, but its royal family and government are having to take greater heed of sections of its population which are hostile - particularly to the continued US military presence on Saudi soil. If the Saudi Arabian oilfields ever did fall under the control of forces hostile to the Western powers, oil supplies and prices would once again pose a major threat to economic prosperity across all of the advanced economies.

In the past a group of countries which belong to an organisation called OPEC has used the West's dependence on imported oil to exert great influence over the global economy.

OPEC: The Organisaton of Petroleum Exporting Countries (OPEC) tries to operate as a cartel - an association of independent producers formed to regulate the price and other sale conditions of the product they offer. OPEC reached the height of its power in the 1970s. Its members banded together to restrict output of oil, adding to the shortages caused by military conflict in the Middle East.

OPEC MEMBERS IN 2001

Algeria	Nigeria
Indonesia	Quatar
Iran	Saudi Arabia
Iraq	UAE
Kuwait	Venezuela
Libya	

Source: www.opec.org

In the short term the demand for oil is relatively inelastic with respect to price. People found it difficult to adjust their use of oil and simply paid up to maintain their lifestyles - using their cars, heating homes with oil, etc. Businesses had similar difficulty in reducing the quantity of oil they used because they were locked into particular industrial processes, and couldn't easily switch to other fuels. This enabled OPEC to charge higher oil prices and maintain sales - thus increasing their revenues and profits.

In the longer term, of course, high oil prices act as an incentive for consumers to buy fuel-efficient cars and heating systems, and for industry to switch to other types of fuel for industrial processes and electricity production. This tends to make the demand for oil more price elastic in the long run, reducing the power of OPEC to force prices up by restricting supply.

NON-OPEC OIL PRODUCTION

After a 'good' start, in which the OPEC cartel appeared to exercise great power over the world market for oil, its influence has declined. This is partly because its members often cheat. They meet as a group to agree production cuts which will force the world oil price upwards. Each country accepts a quota specifying their maximum output in the coming months. They observe the effect of OPEC's announcement of production cuts pushing up the oil price - and then individual countries are tempted to cash in by exporting more than they are supposed to. Once the commodity markets realise this, the price falls again.

OPEC's power to act as a cartel and control oil prices has been further undermined by rapid growth in production during the 1980s and 1990s from non-OPEC countries. Britain, Norway and Russia, for example, are important producers, but they are not OPEC members. Russia, in particular, has added over one million barrels a day to its oil output between 1999 and 2001. It is now the world's second largest oil producer, with a daily output of over seven million barrels.

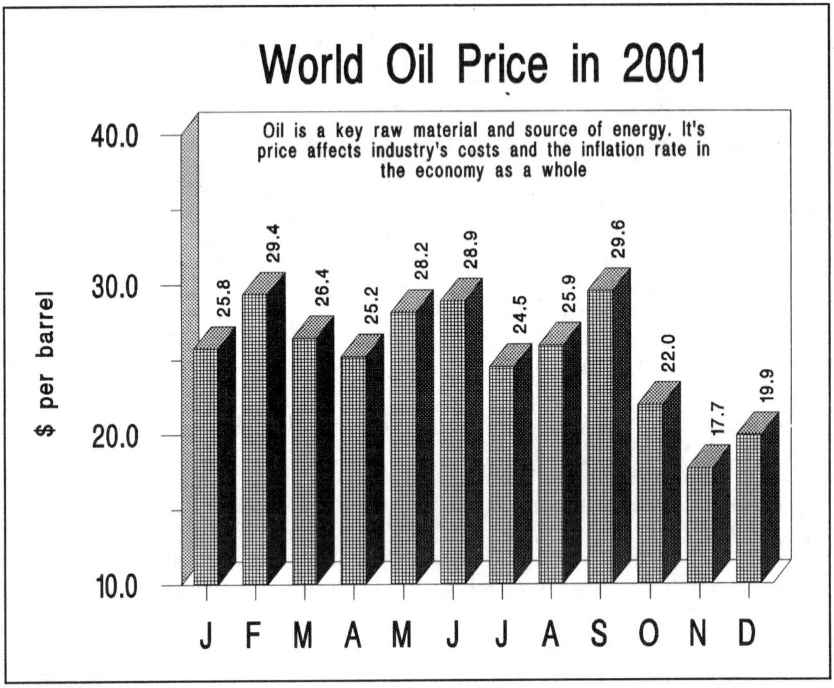

OPEC has set a target price range of $22-28 per barrel and says that this balances the needs of oil producing and consuming nations. However, during the autumn of 2001, after the immediate effects of the September 11 terrorist attacks had abated, OPEC was powerless to prevent the world oil price crashing through the floor of this price band. This was largely due to the attitude of the Russian government, which refused to instruct its oil companies to reduce their output. Later, in December 2001, OPEC members did agree production cuts of 1.5 million barrels a day to try to shore up the world oil price. Russia appeared to have a change of heart and agreed cuts of its own as part of its discussions with OPEC.

This latest action will be an important test of OPEC credibility. If its members, or Russia, cheat and exceed production quotas, OPEC will be seen to be powerless. If, on the other hand, they do succeed in driving the price of oil upwards, all of the old macroeconomic concerns about the potential recessionary consequences for the world economy could resurface. OPEC could once again become a threat to the industrial nations' growth prospects.

BUSINESS BRIEFING - OIL

A low oil price is mixed news for UK industry:

OIL COMPANIES: Companies such as BP and Shell lose out from low oil prices. They have relatively static production costs, making big profits when the price of oil is high and much lower profits when it falls. BP says it makes adequate returns on its investments in oil production when the price is $16 a barrel or higher.

OTHER BUSINESSES: Large scale users of oil generally welcome low oil prices because production costs are reduced. Road haulage businesses, other transport operators and electricity generators benefit strongly from depressed global oil markets.

UK ECONOMY: As a net exporter of oil, low prices adversely affect the UK's balance of payments, but favourably affect the inflation outlook since energy costs are reduced.

TECHNOLOGY SLUMP

If the world economy has appeared to be sliding from boom into recession, the reversal of fortunes for technology industries is even greater. Technology, media and telecoms (TMT) industrial sectors have experienced a dramatic worldwide bubble of development and over-investment in recent years, which has burst and deflated in savage and damaging fashion.

THE NEW ECONOMY

Such has been the excitement about the role of technolgy in recent years that economists and business analysts have distinguished between the ***new economy*** and the ***old economy.***

The new economy is a term used to refer to those sectors which have benefited most from technological advance. In particular, it relates to the huge increase in the use of information technolgy and communications (ITC) in business, and particularly focusses on the role of the internet. Some common descriptions of parts of the new economy include:

B2C - Business to consumer uses of the internet for on-line retailing and travel bookings etc.

B2B - Business to business uses of ITC for on-line wholesaling, and the co-ordination of buying consortia to source raw materials and components through the internet.

ISP - Internet service providers such as AOL and Freeserve, with varying levels and speeds of access to the ***information super-highway.***

E-BUSINESS

A revolution is taking place in the way people do business. For years now businesses have used computers for routine tasks such as word processing, invoicing and accounting processes. Manufacturers have used sophisticated computer-aided design/computer-aided manufacturing (CAD/CAM) systems. Small businesses use computer applications such as data bases holding customer records and desk top publishing (DTP) systems. All of this could be described as evolutionary - small improvements which gradually boost business efficiency and product quality. The really revolutionary change, however, is the advent of E-business.

E-business combines the more conventional computing discussed above with internet technologies. It creates completely new ways of working, such as:

- Buying and selling goods 'on-line' using web sites, a process known as ***e-commerce***. This enables transactions with customers to take place twenty-four hours a day, seven days a week, fifty-two weeks a year, and can involve secure credit card transactions for easy reliable payment.
- Sharing of information and communicating effectively within the business and across supply chains. For example, two designers working on related projects at offices or factories hundreds or thousands of miles apart can share their ideas, modify each other's drawings and pool their expertise as if they were working in the office next door.
- Web sites offer far more information about a company and its products than was ever available before, and many are interactive. For example, car manufacturer Vauxhall has a site which guides visitors through their entire car buying decision, offering advice and comparison reviews against other models, prices, finance and insurance quotations.

PRODUCTIVITY

Productivity (output per worker) in the ***new economy*** has increased dramatically. This has been very apparent in the ITC industries themselves where efficiency improvements have enabled dramatic cost reductions. During the decade of the 1990s the "real" cost of communications (after allowing for inflation) fell by 35%. The cost of computing and communications equipment has fallen even more rapidly. Economists at Lloyds TSB calculate that by August 2000 the average price of these items was only 25% of their 1990 level in 'real' terms. Even this illustration conceals the true magnitude of these gains since, as any long term user of computers will testify, the power and quality of equipment has also advanced in leaps and bounds.

Falling costs of ITC equipment and the discovery of new business applications has encouraged widespread use in industry and commerce. Many have become fully fledged e-businesses. Others have used the new technologies selectively, but overall the effect has been to accelerate productivity and raise the trend growth in production capacity.

The USA has been in the forefront of the ITC revolution and has benefited most from productivity improvements. From 1995 to 1999 US growth averaged 4.4% per annum, better than that of most other advanced industrial economies, and better than its own performance at any time in the previous twenty years. Of course, this impressive growth rate was not just caused by productivity growth (which boosted the total or ***aggregate*** supply of the US economy). It was also dependent on a business investment boom and a consumer boom which ensured that total or ***aggregate*** demand also grew at a breathtaking rate.

THE TECHNOLOGY MARKETS CRASH

The crash which has befallen the technology sector worldwide can be seen most obviously in the well reported slump in share values. With the biggest hi-tech sector in the world, the USA led the way in establishing a specialised market for technology shares - the NASDAQ.

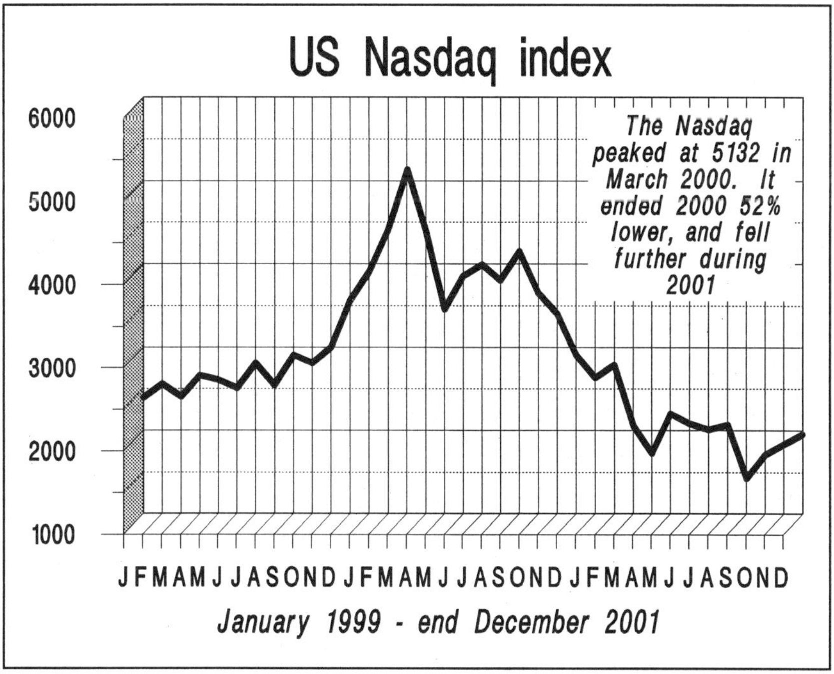

The Nasdaq does not contain just internet-related dot.com companies, but it was the frenzied buying of these and other IT businesses which caused a more general boom on almost any share connected with high technology. During the subsequent crash, major businesses such as Microsoft, Intel, Motorola and Yahoo saw their share prices slump. Poor results in the computer manufacturing sector caused investors to sell Apple, Dell and other leading shares. Telecommunications companies such as America's AT&T and Britain's BT slumped. However, it was the dot.com leaders of the boom which had furthest to fall.

Between the autumn of 1998 and the spring of 2000 the average internet share value rose 800% on the Nasdaq, but then crashed back by approximately the same factor in 2000/2001. This was a classic ***bubble*** market where expectation of quick returns and soaring profits massively outstripped reality. Once investors came to their senses and realised that many technology companies could never be expected to make the level of profits implied by their share prices, they scrambled to sell and the crash gained momentum.

Whilst the US economy and the Nasdaq held centre stage, similar, if less spectacular, stories were unfolding elsewhere. In the UK technology, media and telecoms (TMT) shares fell by 68% between March 2000 and June 2001. Over the same period, a relatively small number of shares defined as "internet" stocks fell by an amazing 98%.

BOO.COM

Boo.com, the online sports fashion retailer, is one of the most celebrated casualties of the technology slump. At one point it was regarded as a glamourous example of dot.com success. Boo was one of the best known names in internet retailing, and supporters believed that this brand recognition would be crucial in winning a large share of a market which they expected to display explosive growth.

Unfortunately, Boo's founders, Kaysa Leander and Ernst Malmsten, managed to burn through £70 million of investors' money in just eighteen months. Most of this went on marketing and genuine business costs, but a fortune was also spent on Concorde flights, Learjet charters and even on twelve Gurkha bodyguards to protect the flamboyant duo.

Boo collapsed in May 2000, but by October it was back, the brand, logo and internet domain name having been bought for a "mere" £250,000 by Fashionmall.com, a surviving dot.com retailer. At its relaunch the company employed nine people, compared with 300-400 during its previous incarnation.

The new Boo.com operates on a different business model. Instead of stocking and selling items directly, the new company acts as a portal through which customers can access a variety of web sites selling what are described as "extraordinary" products.

Meanwhile, Malmsten has turned his hand to publishing and has written a book about his experiences called ***Boo Hoo: a Dotcom Story***, published by Random House Business Books.

ONLINE GROCERIES

Online ordering of groceries, which are then delivered to your door, has not caught on as quickly as internet gurus had predicted. In the USA Webvan, a well known internet grocer, devoured $1 billion (£700 million) of investment before collapsing during summer 2001.

In Britain, established retailers are experimenting with online grocery businesses. Tesco is the market leader, delivering 70,000 orders a week. It does this from existing stores, which serve the needs of twelve million customers a week. Sainsbury serves its online customers from massive ***picking centres.*** These are huge warehouses where online orders are processed. However, the limited growth of demand for these services has put the viability of the relatively high-cost picking centre model into question.

In 1996 Anderson Consulting forecast that online ordering with home delivery would grow rapidly to 20% of the UK grocery market. In 2001, it had reached only 1%. However, Verdict, the retail consultancy firm, still predicts growth to almost 6% by 2006.

MEDIA

The media sector, and in particular ITV, has been hit by a severe decline in advertising. This is partly due to the global downturn - advertising is very sensitive to the phases of the business cycle. It has also, on this occasion, been caused by a slump in dot.com advertising from collapsing internet companies which had spent fortunes trying to build their brand image.

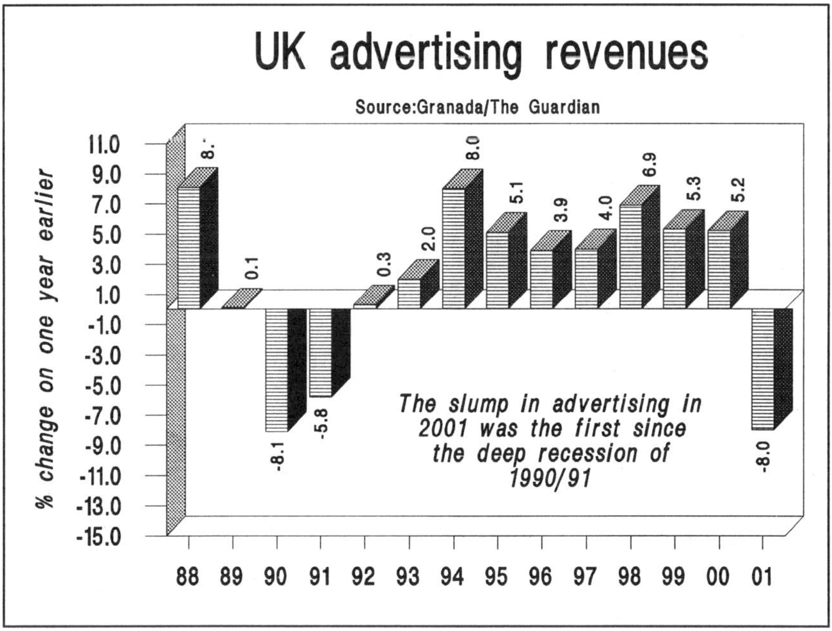

Mobile phone operators have also retrenched. They need less advertising because they have changed their strategies. Instead of expensive campaigns to win new customers they are more committed now to retention and generating improved revenues from their existing client base.

TELECOMS

Telecommunications companies throughout Europe have been caught up in the technology boom and slump in a very big way. These are some of the continent's biggest businesses, and they have seriously over-invested in:

- Cable capacity to meet the needs of internet service providers.
- Capacity to massively expand mobile telecoms services.
- Third generation (3G) licences to permit individual companies to offer advanced mobile telecom, video and internet services in the future.
- Acquisitions of smaller rivals and a wide variety of technology companies which they mistakenly believed would yield good profits in the years ahead.

TELECOMS DEBT RINGS ALARM BELLS

Accumulated debt of leading national telecoms utilities (billion euros)

	January 2000	**January 2001**
Telecom Italia	9	19
BT	14	48
Deutsche Telekom	39	56
France Telecom	19	61

Source: The Guardian/Standard & Poors

The scale of these debt problems, combined with stagnating revenues caused by the global economic slowdown, have undermined confidence in the telecoms sector. 3G licences and investments have added a further area of massive uncertainty, since the technology is as yet untested and nobody knows how popular the new services will become.

Share prices have suffered. France Telecom (which now owns Orange) soared to 220 euros during the boom, but fell to 50 euros by mid 2001. In the UK giant players such as BT and Vodafone came under strong selling pressure. Smaller companies fared much worse. Colt Telecoms, for example, fell from over £35 per share to 60p within two years.

MARCONI: One of Britain's best known and long established technology businesses has performed disastrously in the recent downturn. Marconi used to benefit from lucrative defence contracts - manufacturing electronics equipment for aircraft, ships and weapons systems. More recently, Marconi's directors took the ill-timed decision to switch almost entirely into the manufacture of telecoms equipment. Orders have collapsed, sales are down

20% compared to 2000, and in the six months to September 2001 Marconi made a trading loss of £222 million. However, **overall** losses for this period were a shocking £5.1 billion because accountants have decided to write off over-inflated book values of companies Marconi had acquired.

VODAFONE: Britain's largest mobile telecoms provider has also made an astonishing loss during the first half of 2001. Though Vodafone generated a trading profit of £3 billion during this period, the cost of its ambitious acquisiton programme left it with a net loss of £8.5 billion - one of the largest deficits in UK corporate history.

GLOBALISATION

The globalisation of the world economy is a process in which economic and business decisions are increasingly taken in the context of international free trade and mobile investment funds.

Globalisation is highly controversial. Traditionally it has been seen by economists, business analysts and western governments as "a good thing". Free trade enables countries to specialise - to produce those goods and services where they have a ***competitive advantage.*** Economics textbooks show that world output can be increased if each country specialises in this way, and then trades.

In business, globalisation dramatically increases production and investment possibilities. There is tremendous excitement, for example, over China's impending integration into the global economy through membership of the World Trade Organisation (WTO). China has 1.3 billion consumers - by far the largest emerging market in the world. Globalisation will open up markets for Chinese exports and offer new opportunities for western businesses to trade and invest in one of the fastest growing economic regions of the world.

Globalisation does, however, have bitter oponents:

* The political left in many countries opposes the power which globalisation appears to be giving to multi-national corporations which often dominate small countries and appear to operate outside of the democratic process.
* Anarchists who resent the control over individuals' lives which appears to rest with companies and multi-national organisations such as the WTO.
* Trade unionists in advanced industrial nations who see production shifting to foreign lands where wages are pitifully low and child labour is used to gain a competitive advantage.
* Farmers, particularly in the European Union (EU), who see globalisation as a threat to the agricultural subsidies on which their way of life depends.

WORLD'S LARGEST CORPORATIONS IN 2000

Rank	Company	Country of origin	Revenues ($billion)
1	Exxon Mobil	USA	210
2	Wal-Mart	USA	193
3	General Motors	USA	184
4	Ford	USA	181
5	Daimler Chrysler	Germany	150
6	Royal Dutch-Shell	UK/Netherlands	149
7	BP	UK	148
8	General Electric	USA	129
9	Mitsubishi	Japan	126
10	Toyota	Japan	121

Source: Sunday Times/Fortune 500

* Environmentalists who believe that globalisation, which favours the least cost producer, is undermining attempts to reduce pollution and is causing other forms of environmental destruction.

This resentment against globalisation has brought protestors from the above groups into angry and sometimes violent confrontation with world leaders in recent times, particularly when they have met together to discuss a new round of global trade talks to continue the work of GATT and its successor body, the WTO, which have underpinned globalisation over the past fifty years.

GATT

The General Agreement on Tariffs and Trade (GATT) was established in 1948. Its members met periodically to negotiate free trade agreements and reduce barriers to imports and exports.

On the key issue of tariffs, GATT was immensely successful. At the close of World War II average industrial tariffs stood at 40% - a major deterrent to world trade. At each of the GATT "rounds" of talks - Geneva (1947), Annecy (1948), Torquay (1950), Geneva (1956), Dillon (1060-61), Kennedy (1964-67) and Tokyo (1973-79) - tariffs came tumbling down. By the mid-1980s they averaged just over 5%. For the world's nine largest industrial markets they stood at only 4.7% in 1993.

THE URUGUAY ROUND: The last round of GATT negotiations was launched in 1986 at Punta del Este in Uruguay. It was the most ambitious and complicated round to date, with twenty-eight separate accords which extended fair trade principles for the first time ever to agriculture, textiles, foreign investment, intellectual property rights and certain kinds of services.

WORLD TRADE ORGANISATION

From 1st January 1995 GATT was replaced by the World Trade Organisation (WTO). This has stronger powers than GATT to monitor and police the world trade system. It is dedicated to the promotion of free trade and the demise of illegal forms of trade protectionism.

Whilst disputes still arise, the WTO has proved to be a valuable mechanism for avoiding trade conflict. The WTO was pivotal in helping to avoid, for example, a long running battle between the USA and EU over the importation of bananas from developing into all-out trade warfare.

SEATTLE TALKS

After years of relatively quiet orderly work at the WTO, an attempt to launch a new round of world trade talks in 1999 ended in failure and chaos.

Representatives of 135 nations attended week-long talks in Seattle (USA) with the intention to launch a new round of trade liberalisation. This was intended to pave the way for further measures to achieve even freer trade between nations and build on the successes of earlier GATT rounds.

Right from the outset, however, many poorer countries had been arguing that it was pointless to introduce new trade liberalisation measures when so much work still needed to be done to fully implement the agreements reached under the Uruguay Round.

Delegates to the talks were furious about the US trying to link labour standards to trade agreements, believing that this would be used by the richer countries to put up legally enforceable barriers to imports from poorer countries. Under these circumstances they were not inclined to open up their own economies to foreign investment in growth sectors such as telecommunications, or agree to new controls to stamp out counterfeit goods and piracy of intellectual property (such as computer software and music CDs). African and Caribbean countries in particular stood firm on these issues. Agriculture was also a further area where the talks failed. The USA pressed the EU to reduce its food export subsidies further than it was prepared to consider.

PROTEST DEMONSTRATIONS: The meeting in Seattle was seized upon by many kinds of protest groups which dislike globalisation and wished to demonstrate against further trade liberalisation. Seattle became a battle-ground between protesters and the police - creating a dreadful background for discussions within the trade conference halls. As the protests turned violent, hundreds of demonstrators were arrested in the worst trouble of its kind the US had seen since the anti-Vietnam War marches of the 1960s.

GENOA SUMMIT

Though not strictly part of the WTO process, the 2001 G8 summit in Genoa, Italy, reminded the world about the depth of feeling about globalisation. The summit - a meeting of the world's eight most powerful nations - provoked even more violent protests than those seen in Seattle. A mix of anarchist-led fighting with over-zealous policing left one protestor dead and parts of Genoa in flames.

TRIUMPH IN QATAR

Against all odds, trade ministers from the 142 members of the WTO agreed, in November 2001, to launch a new round of trade liberalisation talks over the coming years. The negotiations will be very difficult and complex, but it is hoped that by 2005 a new deal will be agreed to expand free trade and boost the fortunes of the world economy.

Meeting at Doha in the Gulf state of Qatar, some delegates appear to have connected the need to start a new round of trade talks with the threat to global stability caused by the September 11 terrorist attacks on the USA. UK Trade Secretary, Patricia Hewitt, said that the decision to start the new trade round would give a badly needed boost to world economic confidence and would ***signal the determination of the world's community to fight terror with trade as well as arms.***

In a surprise development, the EU made a major concession on agriculture, which had threatened to prevent progress on the talks. Its negotiators agreed to reductions, with the view to phasing out, of agricultural export subsidies. These are widely seen as unfair, particularly by poorer agricultural countries, but the EU had previously resisted their inclusion in the new

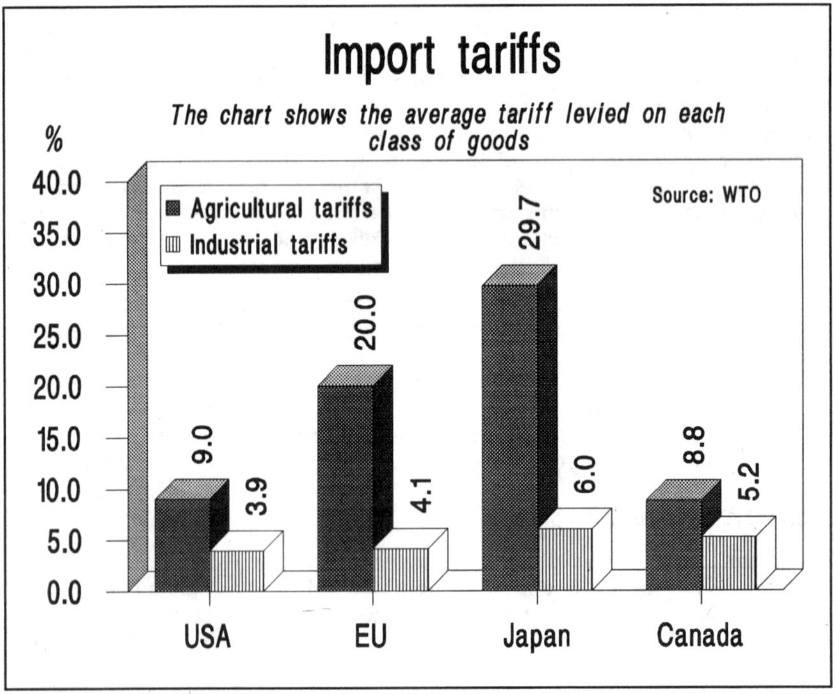

round of talks. In return, the EU received assurances that environmental protection would be given much needed attention in the future negotiations.

The EU and other heavily protected agricultural markets will also come under pressure to dismantle the system of import tariffs which shelter their own producers from the forces of global competition.

EU farmers will shudder to hear this, but logically there is a case to be made for greater attention to agriculture by the WTO. Successive rounds of GATT talks drove down tariff levels and other forms of trade protection on industrial goods, but left agriculture relatively unscathed. As the diagram shows, there is considerable scope to reduce the barriers to agricultural trade, though the process of achieving this is unlikely to be universally popular.

BUSINESS START-UPS

Business start-ups can be the source of great potential for growth and dynamism in local, regional and national economies. Public policy has focussed for many years on the need to nurture small firms in general, but more recently the government and its agencies have concentrated particularly on new business formation.

Small firms are regarded as important because of the contribution they make to wealth creation and employment. If small firms are defined as employing 0-49 employees, government statistics show that they comprise 99.1% of all UK businesses and 44.7% of employment.

Gordon Brown, Chancellor of the Exchequer, has drawn attention to the potential benefits of small business start-ups. He has called for a campaign to create 250,000 new small firms to match rates of business formation found in the USA. Brown says:

* A much larger proportion of the adult population in America are starting new businesses compared with the UK.
* The key to neighbourhood renewal is not more benefit offices but more businesses.
* Britain's national culture should be changed in favour of enterprise, and this should start, not in company boardrooms, but in our schools and colleges.

A growing number of young people do, it seems, dream of starting their own business. Shell Livewire is an organisation which gives advice to people under thirty years of age starting up in business. During 2000 over 80,000 aspiring entrepreneurs (average age twenty-two) contacted Livewire - mostly interested in web design or IT consultancy opportunities.

The UK already has 3.7 million small and medium sized enterprises (0-250 employees). Their number has increased by over 50% since the early 1980s. The Federation of Small Businesses welcomes government proposals to foster

250,000 new start-ups, but argues for a degree of caution. The Federation says that currently two out of every three new firms fails within three years. In order to be successful, Brown's initiative will need to provide a strong level of support for businesses once they have come into being.

Fortunately, much attention is being given to the forms of help which budding entrepreneurs can access:

SMALL BUSINESS SERVICE: The Small Business Service (SBS), which co-ordinates the Business Links offices around the country, is able to provide help for individuals developing their business plan. This help has been extended to £2,000 per case in the 2001 Budget.

COMMUNITY INVESTMENT FUNDS: These have been set up by combining government cash (through the SBS) with private investment to form a pool of around £500 million available for small firms with excellent business concepts, who have not been able to raise sufficient finance from the banks. There are 180 funds, such as "Salford Money Line"; "Developing Strathclyde"; "Sheffield Enterprise Agency"; and "Street UK", serving Bradford and Newcastle.

UNIVERSITIES: Higher Education institutions are increasingly turning themselves into ***business incubators*** to identify and nurture start-up opportunities, particularly for their own staff and students.

Research programmes in universities, particularly in sciences, generate ***intellectual property*** (IP). This can be exploited to produce a financial return by patenting brilliant new concepts and then selling licences to private sector partners who turn the IP into new products. Alternatively, the universities can "spin out" new companies of their own to utilise the IP and bring new concepts directly to the market. Academics in several universities can gain access to the University Challenge Fund (UCF), which is nothing to do with the popular BBC quiz programme. It is a multi-million pound fund to help professors and their staff to develop and prove their business concepts so that they can spin out new companies, often with further financial support from specialist investors called Venture Capitalists.

Students can also benefit from entrepreneurship schemes as they approach graduation. The government has introduced Science Enterprise Challenge, which develops centres of excellence in the education of science and technology students in entrepreneurial skills. The University of Nottingham Institute for Enterprise and Innovation (UNIEI) has, for example, been set up as part of this scheme to boost science-based entrepreneurship in the East Midlands.

Regional Development Agencies (RDAs) have been concentrating their efforts on the development of 'clusters' of concentrated economic activity. They have at their disposal the Innovative Clusters Fund (ICF) which pays for the establishment of physical incubator facilities - typically, modern industrial facilities, offices or studios attached to universities to house spin-out businesses. York and Nottingham have, for example, established bio-technology incubators, whilst the University of Lincoln is developing a media

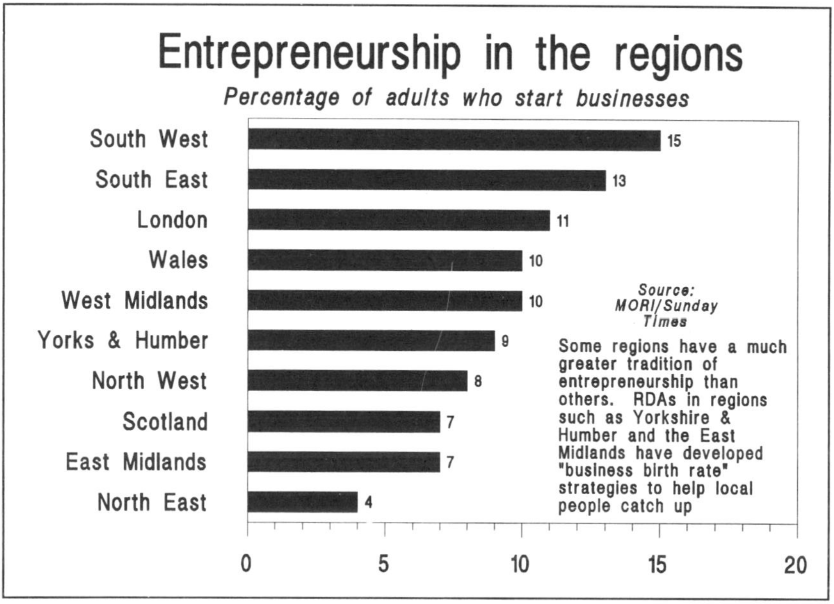

incubator with ICF assistance to accommodate businesses formed by its media and computing graduates.

BUSINESS ANGELS: Help for start-ups and expanding small businesses does not just come from the government and the public sector. Banks and venture capital companies are major sources of finance. Some wealthy individuals - often successful entrepreneurs in their own right - also provide financial backing and much needed strategic business advice. These ***business angels*** play an important role in extending finance for promising businesses with high growth potential, usually in exchange for a share in their equity capital and future profits.

The National Business Angels Network (NBAN) claims that there are 20,000 business angels operating in the UK. They tend to be found in areas where there are intense clusters of entrepreneurial activity - for example, in London, Oxford and Edinburgh.

INNOVATION

Innovation is defined by the Department of Trade and Industry (DTI) as ***the successful exploitation of new ideas.*** Innovation is not the same as invention, since many new ideas never progress beyond the drawing board. Businesses need to gain access to inventions or new ideas, ***and*** find ways of using them successfully to improve competitiveness, for innovation to have occurred.

The European Commission is keen to encourage innovation, and has published an ***Innovation Scoreboard*** to show how individual countries are performing.

INNOVATION SCOREBOARD

The EU scores member states against seventeen separate indicators in four areas:

* Human resources
* Knowledge creation
* Transmission and application of new knowledge
* Innovation finance, output and markets.

The overall results are summarised into an innovation index, and these are shown in the chart below.

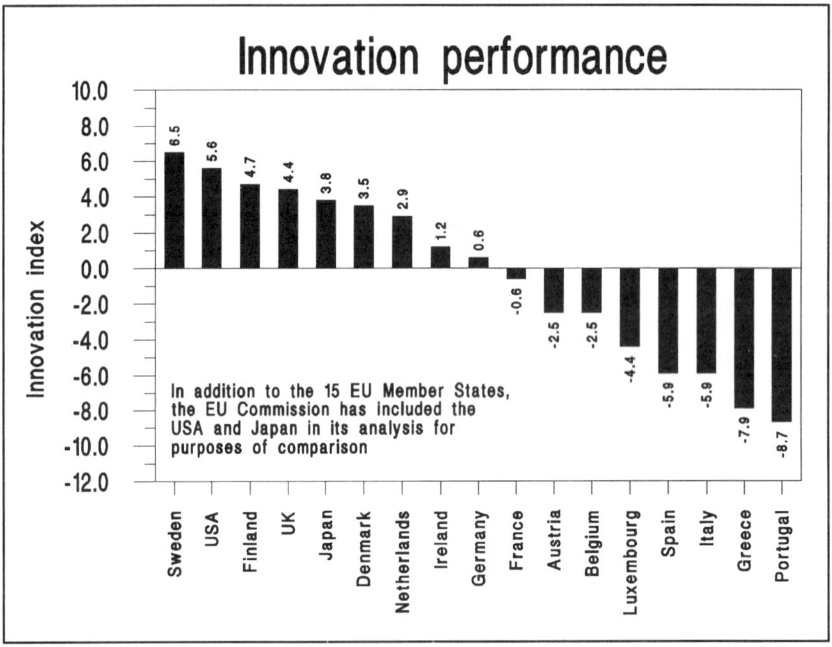

The Innovation Scoreboard casts doubt on the commonly held view that Britain is sadly lacking in innovation. In fact, the UK performs better in the overall ranking than any other large EU economy. Only Finland and Sweden do better. The USA outperforms the UK on innovation, but Japan does slightly worse.

Innovation is a complex process, and the UK performs better in some aspects than in others.

UK RELATIVE PERFORMANCE IN INNOVATION

BETTER THAN EU AVERAGE

- Output of science and engineering graduates
- Population with tertiary education
- Lifelong learning
- Employment in hi-tech services
- Patents per head of population
- Venture capital expenditure
- Home internet access
- Hi-tech value added

WORSE THAN EU AVERAGE

- SME innovation (In-house)
- Innovation expenditure
- Employment in hi-tech manufacturing
- Public sector expenditure on R&D
- Capital investment

Source: European Innovation Scoreboard: EU Commission, 2001

Whilst the UK performs well in innovation compared to the EU average, there are two important areas where we fall short of our US and Japanese competitors:

BUSINESS EXPENDITURE ON R&D: In the UK private sector business expenditure on research and development is 1.2% of national GDP, exactly the same as the European average. In the USA the comparable figure is 1.98% and in Japan 2.18%, indicating a much larger contribution from the corporate sector.

PATENTS: Patents are taken out by companies and research institutes to protect their ***intellectual property*** - the valuable ideas they have created. US and Japanese patenting activity is much higher than it is in the UK or across Europe in general. Internationally, US hi-tech patenting in Europe is seven times higher than European patenting in the US. More than any other factor, this points to a higher level of commercial awareness amongst researchers and their employers in the USA than in Europe. In Sweden, for example, which tops the Innovation Scoreboard, R&D expenditures are an even higher percentage of GDP than in the USA or Japan, but patenting activity is lower.

RESEARCH AND DEVELOPMENT

Research can be ***pure*** or ***applied.*** Pure research is a 'blue skies' quest for technical knowledge with no specific end in view. This is normally conducted in university laboratories and in the very largest of businesses, which have the resources to take a long term view and can wait for financial returns. Applied research is more commonplace in business, and aims to solve particular problems - finding new production techniques and product improvements. Finally, to complete the R&D process, products have to be prepared for the marketplace. Usually prototypes (experimental products) are manufactured and tested before full scale production begins.

R&D is, as we have seen earlier, an important aspect of innovation in which the UK underperforms. However, further analysis shows that there are different rates of R&D in different industrial sectors.

R&D EXPENDITURES IN 2001

Sector	Proportion of total UK R&D (%)	R&D intensity* UK (%)	R&D intensity international (%)
IT hardware	7.5	6.2	8.1
Automotive	5.5	4.2	4.0
Pharmaceuticals	37.7	14.8	12.8
Electronics	4.3	3.0	5.8
Chemicals	2.7	1.4	4.1
Software	4.8	4.2	14.3
Aerospace	10.0	7.7	4.4
Engineering	2.8	1.3	2.8
Telecoms	2.9	1.0	1.8
Health	1.7	7.2	5.3
Food processors	5.8	1.6	1.8
Oil and gas	4.3	0.3	0.4
Other	1.0	2.1	4.2
Total	**100.0**	**2.1**	**4.2**

* R&D intensity = R&D expenditure as a percentage of total sales

Source: Department of Trade & Industry/The Independent

Two sectors, pharmaceuticals and aerospace, dominate UK R&D activity, accounting for almost half of all recorded expenditure. These are also sectors where the R&D intensity is greater in the UK than it is across the world as a whole. Health accounts for a small proportion of UK R&D, but the intensity is still higher than it is internationally. In all of the other sectors the UK underperforms compared with the international average. Overall, across all sectors, the research intensity in the UK is 2.1%, only half of the international average.

Unlike the giants of the pharmaceutical world, such as GLaxoSmithKline and AstraZeneca, Britain's SMEs are mostly averse to R&D. In the UK just 4% of companies invest 10% or more of their turnover in R&D. For the USA the comparable figure is 27%.

Lord Sainsbury, the government's Science and Innovation Minister, says that, whilst the levels of business expenditure on R&D are rising steadily, the UK will need to do better to remain internationally competitive. He says ***Too many companies still fail to recognise that R&D is a key driver of growth.***

In recent Budgets the government has increased tax incentives for SMEs to undertake R&D, but the effects of this have yet to show up in the published statistics for actual R&D performance.

REGULATION AND RED TAPE

Businesses in the UK, and in Europe in general, operate under an extensive and detailed regime of government and local authority regulations. Governments in other parts of the world, such as the USA and Asia, also regulate businesses to some degree, but have a reputation for applying a 'lighter touch' than their European counterparts.

WHY DO GOVERNMENTS REGULATE?

It is tempting to criticise all business regulation as government meddling which holds back entrepreneurs and damages growth prospects. For most people this would be a huge exaggeration. Health and safety, the environment, racial and gender discrimination and monopoly power are all examples of important business issues which need to be regulated.

During the 1980s the Conservative Prime Minister, Margaret Thatcher, made a big issue of ***deregulation,*** reducing controls on bus services, telecommunications and many other industries.

The present Labour government says it is serious about creating a vibrant business climate to foster the development of small firms, but many critics argue that it is creating too much ***red tape.***

RED TAPE

Red tape is a term in common use for the irritating restrictions which often result from regulation. This might typically involve filling in countless forms, keeping records, preparing for inspections by regulators and keeping track of new legislation. Even before we take into account the fundamental restriction of business activity implied by regulation, this proliferation of red tape imposes heavy costs, particularly on smaller firms where owners or managers have to cope with it as well as run their company.

The present Labour government is the most business-friendly in the history of British politics. Labour politicians cultivated business contacts during the later years of opposition, received donations from industry in the run-up to the 1997 election, and involve business leaders in many think tanks and policy making bodies. The Prime Minister, Tony Blair, is comfortable in addressing the Confederation of British Industry (CBI) conference, but at his November 1999 appearance he felt obliged to distance himself from 'over the top regulation'. ***Blair plans war on red tape*** read the headlines as the Prime Minister faced up to the challenge to his government's popularity amongst the business community created by the perceived increase in red tape.

Two years on, however, and complaints about red tape are at an all-time high. A recent survey by the Federation of Small Businesses showed that 83% of its members were dissatisfied by the volume and complexity of legislation they had to deal with. In a further study by the EU Commission, the UK was regarded as the worst place to do business in Europe because of our ***rigid enforcement of business regulations.*** This is almost certainly a gross exaggeration since, for example, the UK attracts far more inward investment than any other EU country. However, it does further reinforce the concerns that entrepreneurship and business growth might be stifled by regulation.

The British Chambers of Commerce (BCC) estimates that the costs of regulation are soaring and have reached £15 billion a year. The BCC's main concerns are over:

- UK adoption of the EU Working Time Directive (cost £7.66 billion)
- The Data Protection Directive (cost £3.1 billion)
- EU Pollution Directive (cost £1.6 billion)
- Administration of the Minimum Wage (£2.4 billion in extra pay for low wage earners ***plus*** £0.7 billion in business administration costs)

Other ***red tape*** burdens are said to be the costs to businesses of administering the stakeholder pension, welfare reforms, the disability discrimination act, the working families tax credit, study and training provision for young people, and the part-time workers' directive.

Looking through the above list, many readers will be able to find measures that they support. After all, isn't it important to reduce pollution, to encourage saving for retirement, to avoid discrimination, etc, etc? The point is, though, that a flood of new legislation has heaped so many new responsibilities on businesses that it could be damaging their competitiveness.

BETTER REGULATION TASK FORCE

The government has promised to be more sensitive to the business impacts of regulation in the future. It has a ***Better Regulation Task Force*** which examines regulation from five perspectives:

- transparency - are the rules easy to understand?
- proportionality - are the burdens imposed reasonable compared with the objective and potential benefits?
- accountability - are officials who implement the regulations answerable for their actions?

* targeting - are regulations directed to the areas of business where they are most necessary?
* consistency - are they applied logically and fairly in all situations?

SMALL BUSINESS SERVICE: The government has created a Small Business Service (SBS) which owes its origins to the successful Small Business Administration operating in the USA since the 1950s. The SBS will build upon the one-stop-shop concept pioneered by Business Links in the UK, and offer an even more comprehensive array of business support services. This will include a strong emphasis on helping business to cope with regulation. The Chief Executive of the SBS is intended to provide a strong voice for small business in government circles, and will be in a good position to advise against unnecessarily onerous rules and restrictions.

NEW LEGISLATION

The government needs to strike a difficult balance between new socially progressive laws and the need to protect business competitiveness. In 2001 new legislative proposals were announced to encourage employers to offer flexible hours of work for mothers and fathers with young children under the age of six or disabled children up to eighteen.

The new laws will come into force in 2003 and are intended to strike a better balance between work and family life. However, campaigners for such measures will be disappointed that the new legislation will not provide an absolute legal right for employees to work child-friendly hours. Instead, employers will only have to go through a formal process to consider requests from individual workers to vary their hours. It is estimated that around 500,000 workers a year will be affected and that 80% will have their requests accepted. Employers will be able to refuse to offer flexible hours if they can show that their business would be damaged. Disputes over the implementation of these new rules will be settled by tribunals.

CLIMATE CHANGE

The change in the world's climate, caused by atmospheric warming, is one of the biggest challenges facing the world today. During 2001 there were both failures and successes in beginning to tackle this frighteningly important problem.

GLOBAL WARMING

The earth's atmosphere is warming up. Average global temperatures today are 5°C higher than they were at the end of the last ice age. There is a natural variation in temperatures from one year/decade/century to another, but gradually the evidence has been mounting up to show that we are in a phase of serious warming which cannot be ignored.

The Intergovernmental Panel on Climate Change, sponsored by the United

Nations, predicts a ***worst case*** scenario where average global temperatures rise by a further 6°C over the next one hundred years. Only five years ago the same panel said the worst case would be a rise of 3°C. Since then, additional data has been gathered, showing actual temperatures which exceed any similar string of years for many centuries. Also, scientific understanding of the processes causing global warming has increased, and more realistic computer models have been created to predict future trends.

EFFECTS OF GLOBAL WARMING

The effects of global warming of this scale and severity are potentially devastating:

* Glaciers are already retreating and the polar ice caps thinning, upsetting delicate ecosystems which support wildlife in the Arctic and Antarctic.
* Already there is evidence of increased precipitation and a big rise in weather-related natural disasters, such as those caused by storms and hurricanes.
* Climate change alters growing conditions, and is likely to lead to crop failures in many parts of the world.
* Rising sea levels caused by the melting ice caps threaten countries vulnerable to coastal flooding. Low lying countries such as Bangladesh, and island nations such as the Maldives are at greatest risk.

Poor countries, without the resources to cope with these problems, will be in deep trouble, and we can expect to see huge numbers of refugees trying to escape from the worst affected areas.

GLOBAL WARMING FACT FILE

* Six of the ten hottest years on record for global temperatures were in the 1990s - the other four were in the 1980s.
* Arctic sea ice has, over thirty years, reduced in thickness from three metres to two metres, and the process is accelerating.
* Large pieces of Arctic sea ice are failing to form in the Greenland area as they always have done in the past.
* Carbon dioxide levels, which cause global warming, are at their highest levels for twenty million years.

Ironically, as the world warms up, there is a possibility that Britain and Scandinavia could cool down in equally dramatic fashion. Ocean currents circulate around the Atlantic. The **Gulf Stream**, a warm water current, flows from the tropics northwards and keeps North Western Europe about 5°C warmer than would normally be expected at such latitudes. A return cold water flow, called the **Labrador Current**, takes cold water south. This is equivalent to a submarine river, thirty times the size of the Amazon, which redistributes heat and cold around the planet. This process, which is also known as the **North Atlantic Conveyor**, is showing signs that it is faltering. If it weakens, or switches off completely, temperatures would plunge in Britain and other affected areas as the Gulf Stream effect is lost. Many people mistakenly think that global warming might have pleasant effects - making Britain's climate warmer like the Mediterranean. Under the nightmare scenario just described, our climate would become more like that of Iceland than the South of France!

WHAT CAN BE DONE?

Global warming is man-made. Scientists believe that it is man's economic activities (in particular through atmospheric pollution and the burning of fossil fuels) which are causing the earth to heat up. Carbon dioxide emissions from factories, motor vehicles, power stations and home heating systems are the main problem. These, on a global scale, represent a giant thermal blanket surrounding our planet, which traps heat from the sun causing the atmosphere to warm.

Carbon has been locked in "fossil" fuels, such as coal, oil and natural gas, for millions of years. Then, within a few hundred years, through industrialisation man has extracted these fuels from the earth's crust and released carbon dioxide gases into the atmosphere by burning them.

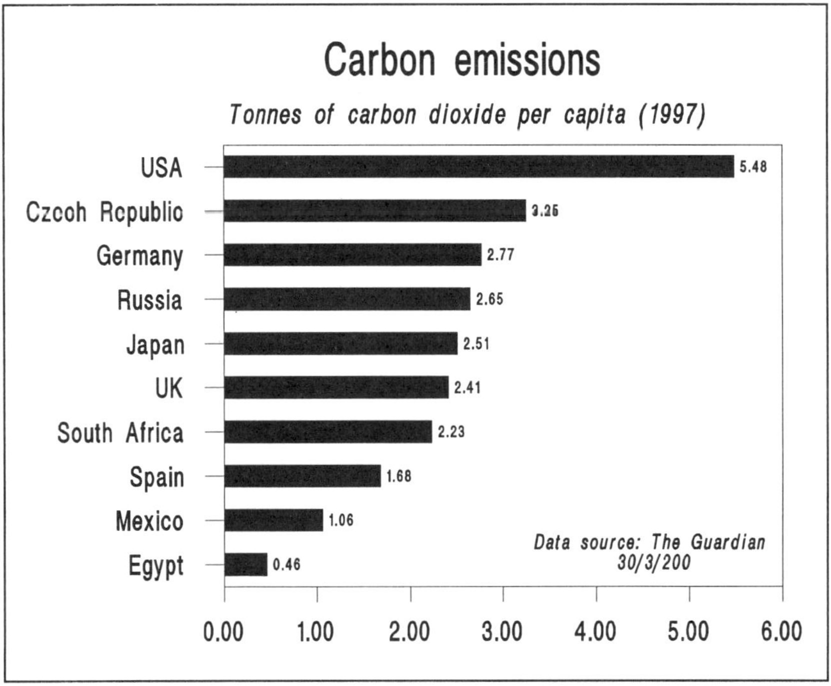

An international group of scientists have worked out that carbon dioxide emissions should be cut back to 60% of 1990 levels worldwide. Even this would not halt global warming immediately, but might limit the damage already being done.

KYOTO: At an international conference in Kyoto, Japan, in 1997 governments agreed to cut back by 5.5% of 1990 emission levels by 2010, but this has proved difficult to implement and in March 2001 the US government abandoned its Kyoto commitments. The USA is by far the largest producer of carbon dioxide, and its unilateral action threatened to destroy the first steps towards a solution to the problem of global warming.

The USA's worries over Kyoto are, to some extent, understandable. Reducing carbon dioxide emissions will mean sacrifices. Americans may have to drive smaller cars, travel less often, and turn down their air conditioning systems to reduce their use of fossil fuels. However, surveys of US consumers show they are also worried about climate change. After all, the Atlantic seaboard, particularly around Florida, is one of the areas threatened most by the growing severity of hurricanes. Critics argue that the Bush administration is out of touch and is obsessed with maintaining economic growth at the expense of climate change. A Texan himself, George W Bush is also said to be unduly influenced by pressure from oil and coal producers who have a vested interest in maintaining high levels of energy consumption.

The costs of reducing carbon emissions might be high for all advanced economies, but the costs of ***not*** reducing them are even higher. The UN has estimated that the cost of reducing emissions over the next ten years will be less than 1% of developed countries' GDP, whereas the cost of doing nothing could eventually be at least 10% to 20% of GDP for those countries. Some environmentalists think that the risks are even higher, with delay leading to unstoppable and catastrophic rates of global warming.

The current situation is dangerous but ***not*** hopeless. Wind power and solar energy are already available. Fuel cell technologies are being developed which should produce plentiful supplies of pollution-free energy. Huge strides can be made in energy conservation if governments have the will to implement them. Even the planting of trees helps because forests represent carbon 'sinks' which remove carbon dioxide from the atmosphere and store it in a less dangerous form.

A DEAL IS DONE

Meeting at Bonn in July 2001, 186 nations ignored America's intransigence and signed the Kyoto Protocol. This included thirty-eight industrialised countries which have all agreed to cut CO^2 emissions and enforce the Kyoto Protocol through their own national laws. The EU has agreed to cut CO^2 emissions by 8% of 1990 levels by 2010, and the UK's target will be 12.5%.

Industrialised countries will be able to claim ***carbon credits*** for planting forests and managing their agriculture in ways which remove CO^2 from the atmosphere. A system of carbon trading will be set up, in which companies which save carbon emissions will be able to sell the carbon credits they earn to others which are unwilling or unable to do so. These companies will then be able to meet the requirements of new laws controlling emissions, but they will still be contributing to the costs of decarbonising the economy in general. In the future, tons of carbon dioxide (saved) will be sold on international commodity markets in the same way as tons of rice or copper. London is expected to become the leading centre managing this global trade.

Readers might think that the system of carbon trading is too 'soft' on polluting companies, but it is actually very efficient in economic terms. It means that those companies which find it easy and cheap to reduce carbon emissions do so, and trade carbon credits with others who would find it very costly to adapt. In the process, the overall target for reduced emissions is met.

A more serious criticism concerns the extent to which the Bonn agreement will reduce global warming. It has been heralded as a great breakthrough - the first international deal to tackle the problem. However, critics argue that the scale of CO^2 reductions are too small, and with the USA remaining free to pollute as usual, the reduction in global temperatures might be as little as one tenth of a degree centigrade. The main hope must be that this is only the start - with much more serious action to follow.

One thing is almost certain - mankind will have to learn to live with global warming as well as control it. There are huge time lags in the natural system, since once CO^2 is generated it stays in the atmosphere for a hundred years. By acting now we are trying to avoid disaster for future generations, but climate change and rising sea levels are here to stay for many decades to come.

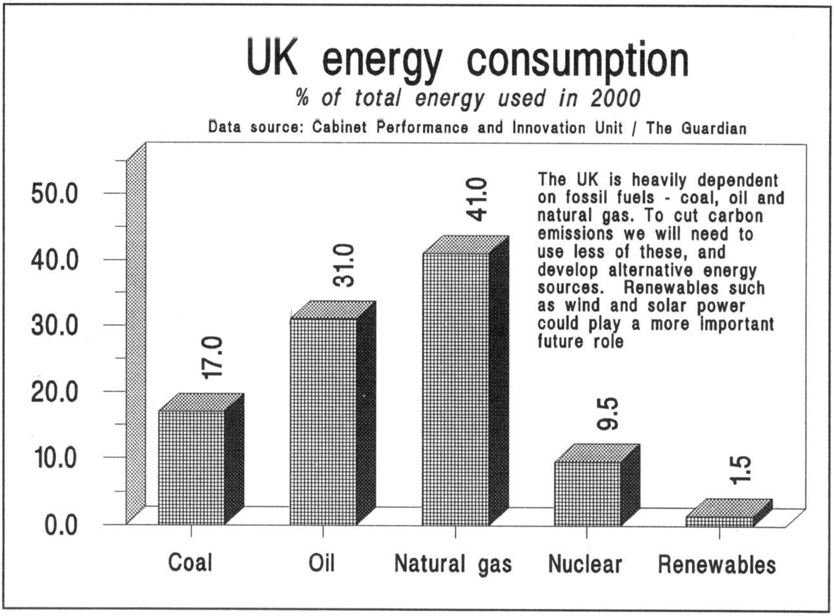

BUSINESS STUDIES UPDATE

BACK ISSUES PACK

FIVE EDITIONS FROM 1997 - 2001

AT THE SPECIAL PRICE OF £10.00 PER PACK

A unique source of information on:

The Single European Currency; Business Trends; Government Economic Policies; Privatisation; Monopolies and Mergers; Retailing; Small Firms; Business Failures; Inward Investment; Human Resources; Trade Unions and Industrial Relations; Asian Financial Crisis and World Trade

***Plus* many other important topics**

PLEASE ORDER USING THE FORM ON PAGE 64

THE SINGLE EUROPEAN CURRENCY

2000 Edition

- **Launch of the Eurozone**
- **Background to the Single Currency**
- **How it relates to the Exchange Rate Mechanism, European Monetary System and the Maastricht Treaty**
- **Business planning for the Euro**
- **The perils of floating exchange rates**
- **The single currency and European regional disparities**
- **Should Britain join the Single Currency?**
- **The National Changeover Plan**

32 pages: first published January 2000: ISBN 1-898837-45-7

Price: £3.00 including p&p (or order as part of a pack - see page 64)

PLEASE ORDER USING THE FORM ON PAGE 64